The first edition was a noble start--but flawed on many levels. My appreciation goes to
Medic. He re-shot all the pictures for this edition using fancy-pants photo equipment. It ... Thank you,
Bruce.

Thank you, as well, to Ben Peterselli. Not only is he our 8th GWHS English Department Chairman, but he also helped to edit
it and work on the layout for this edition. I really appreciate his keen eye.

Should you find errors or omissions, please share them with me. There needs to be a 3rd edition and 4th edition, and so on. I
finally had to stop working in this edition. The first edition took 3 months to write. In contrast, this 2nd edition took 7
months. Please direct comments and corrections to me: steve_wiersum@glenbard.org

Steven Wiersum
English teacher
Sponsor of the Glenbard West High
School Historic Society

Photo by Eric Shelkopf, used with permission

P.S. One day, while casually flipping through the 1942 *Pinnacle*, I happened to look down to glance at
page 92. To my amazement, there was MY last name: Wiersum. It is not a common name. I took a
picture, sent it to my father and, sure enough! I had found a cousin that I did not even know I had. In
fact, I had two, since the Wiersum boy, Joseph, pictured above, had a sister, Henrietta Wiersum, who
graduated from Glenbard High School in 1944, at right. Joseph Wiersum graduated in 1943. What are
the odds?

About Henry J. Firley

This book has been printed as a fund raiser for the Henry J. Firley Award. 100% of all profits from the sale of this book go
directly to the Firley Award. The GWHS English department is deeply grateful for your generous support!

Henry J. Firley was Glenbard West's first English Department Chair. He held that position for
34 years, from 1931 to 1965. Not only did his tenure span several decades, it was though his
efforts that made our school yearbook, *Pinnacle*, possible. He was a teacher, poet, literary
critic, and America's first literary cartographer—in short, a true renaissance man. When Mr.
Firley passed away in 1973, his wife, Mrs. Hazel Firley, donated a sum of money to set up a
writing award in Mr. Firley's name. The Henry J. Firley writing award, created to recognize
originality and excellence in writing, has been given to a
Glenbard West senior since June of 1975. At right, a
caricature of Mr. Firley from his *Pinnacle* Staff.

**If you would like to donate to The Firley Award, please contact Ben Peterselli—a
graduate of GWHS and our 8th English Department Chairman. He can be
reached by calling the school's main switchboard: 630-469-8600**

Dedication

I want to take a moment to dedicate this book to some very special people. This book is dedicated to:

The Glenbard West Boosters. Thank you, thank you for your support! We have used your generous grant to frame over 300 pictures and artifacts, start the GWHS Historic Club, and begin a committee to nominate and honor our distinguished alumni.

Dr. Susan J. Bridge who hired me to teach English starting in the fall of 1994. I still remember her phone call when she awarded me the position. I have always been grateful to her and hope that his book honors the work she did on the history of the school. That extensive volume allowed her to earn her Ed.D. and share the accurate history of GWHS.

Dr. Peter Monaghan who appreciates and loves this school with such awe and respect. If you cherish GWHS, then you cannot do better than to have this man in the principal's office guarding and guiding the school's Pride, Tradition, and Excellence.

Bruce Medic who volunteered to take wonderful pictures of artifacts.

Special thanks to the 1931 editor of *The Glen Bard*, Geraldine Benthey for saving and sharing a box of Glenbard newspapers. What a precious gift!

Allie Dahlgren and Grace Davidson, the first two GWHS Historic Society Club presidents who helped get it started—and kept it going.

The students in the GWHS Historic Society Club who met together for Pizza, Pop, and Preservation. Your energy was so contagious! A special thank you to Katie Cavanagh, Katie Sinta, Ellery DiVenere—class of 2019!

Howard Schwartz, the GWHS art teacher who asked me if I were interested in taking on the role of historian after his retirement.

Bill Ortega, who did so much work on researching the information on the building itself.

Ben Peterselli, who not only graduated from GWHS, but then returned as the English Department Chairman. Who would have thought that, as a sophomore sitting in my wife's English class, he would return to fill Mr. Henry J. Firley's chair? Thank you for your enthusiasm and encouragement as I worked on the book and its materials.

Jim Corso. Mentor. Friend. You sat on the committee to hire me and became such a wonderful friend to me. And did I mention his jokes? Who knew that he could even have a joke about a schnauzer in his repertoire?

Joel Sherr. It was your recommendation that began my search into the history of my school. Wow.

Snub Pritchard, Joe Carlton, and Glenn Reynolds for coming to our Historic Society meetings and helping us with the stories and timelines. You make us proud to be Hilltoppers.

Laura Capel Classen and Steve Edelson. Thank you for all the information and time you shared with me to help piece together the story of Bruce Capel—the Original Hitter.

My wife, Elizabeth Wiersum, who has been teaching English with me at GWHS since I started. She is an amazing teacher, a wonderful friend, and a loving wife.

GLENBARD WEST
HIGH SCHOOL

At left, a 1927 oil painting of Glenbard High School. The original painting hangs in room 428—the Alumni Room

Below, the art glass of Glenbard West High School currently hangs in the Elliott Library. The artist, Kelly Lagerholm, made it for the American Studies class taught by Kath Bergin and Mary Kate Bertane

The History of Glenbard West High School, Second edition. 2019

This book is a compilation of efforts. A majority of the text is taken from a photocopy of Glenbard West High School's history. At this point, the author—or authors-- remain unknown. Former art teacher, Howard Schwartz, may have had a hand in it. He certainly should be credited with taking care of so much historic items such as pictures, photos, art works. Howard's greatest contribution was the work he did to make room 428 an official archive room. The oak bookcases and the display cases are the pinnacle of his effort.

The display cases also lead to the creation of the Glenbard West High School Historic Society. Shortly after Howard approached me to take over the work of Glenbard West's history, I met two students in room 428, Allie Dahlgren and her friend. They were both sophomores.

The three of us were waiting in 428 for some French students. Allie and her friend were in Mme. Callicoat's French class and she had asked if I could meet them in 428 to tell them a little about the history of the school.

As we waited, the girls became fascinated by the photos in Howard's cases. One photo in particular captured their attention. In it, Fred L. Biester, our long-time and beloved principal/superintendent, stood as a group of seniors sat in front of the high school. The photo had been taken before the main entrance was built, but over Fred's right shoulder was the school bell mounted to the building's exterior. I pulled Allie and her friend across the hall from room 428 and showed them the bell, now rusted and silent, but still mounted in the same spot. Somehow, the history of Glenbard hit us all so profoundly that the three of us started a new club, The Glenbard West High School Historic Society.

If you are reading this, you should know that this is the second edition of the GWHS History book. The first book was an attempt to take written and oral history and put it all in one place.

GLENBARD WEST HIGH SCHOOL

A HISTORY

STEVEN WIERSUM

Glenbard West High School
A History

iUniverse books may be ordered through booksellers or by contacting:

iUniverse
1663 Liberty Drive
Bloomington, IN 47403
www.iuniverse.com
1-800-Authors (1-800-288-4677)

ISBN: 978-1-5320-7827-9 (sc)
ISBN: 978-1-5320-7828-6 (e)

Library of Congress Control Number: 2019909611

Print information available on the last page.

iUniverse rev. date: 07/12/2019

Table of Contents

Patch: "G" with Castle Tower. According to 1977 graduate Ed Rhodes, it is "the 1977 Chess Team 'letterman' award, created with a certain amount of seriousness and a certain amount of tongue-in-cheekness to assert the claim that the Chess Team was in fact an interscholastic competitive team. I've got a letter jacket around somewhere with a similar letter on it."

The Four Names of the High School

1915-1921: **Glen Ellyn High School.**

Also referred to as **Glen Ellyn Township High School** the school met in the DuPage County Bank

The first class of Glen Ellyn High School Graduates. Classes met at the DuPage County Bank in 1916. Mr. Holzman was Glenbard High School's first principal.

1922-1958: **Glenbard High School**. It officially became known as GLENBARD on May 15, 1922. Also, Glenbard High School was officially dedicated on May 15, 1923.

1959-Present: **Glenbard West High School.** It became Glenbard West when Glenbard East High School opened

Pictured, at left: At one point, the school was covered in vines. Most of them have since been removed due to the destructive nature of the vines on the brick and mortar.

1890's: The Time Before the Castle

1890's: First high schoolers meet jointly with students from Wheaton, but because Wheaton voters do not want to create a joint high school with Glen Ellyn, Wheaton organizes a high school alone.

1892-1895: Glen Ellyn Hotel stood near, but not on, Honeysuckle Hill. In the photo, you can see Honeysuckle Hill to the right of the hotel. An imposing four-story Victorian structure, it opens in 1892 on a ridge overlooking Lake Ellyn. Located near five mineral springs, the 135-room hotel draws visitors not only from Chicago but from around the country. Water from the springs is touted as an aid to health, and mud from around the springs is packaged and sold as an aid to complexion. A fire destroys the hotel in 1895.

Honeysuckle Hill

To write the history of Glenbard is to pursue the paths of education in this community as it has developed since the first settlers came Westward, erected their log cabins and schoolhouses, and carved a new home on the prairie. As the new America approached maturity, so did its system of education; as the years passed, the one room, eight-grade schoolhouse was deemed inadequate for the technical, specialized world emerging in the late nineteenth century. In the larger cities first, and then in the smaller villages, like Lombard and Glen Ellyn, the high school rose to supplement the existing schools. When a large school was erected in Glen Ellyn in the1890's, one of the rooms was devoted to a "course of advanced study." The project was allowed to lapse, however, because national depression caused financial resources to dwindle.

Despite its short existence, the high school course created interest in secondary education (among the villagers) and is definitely a forerunner of Glenbard. Over the years the possibility of a local high school was raised time and again; the voters consistently refused to ratify any union with Wheaton in this endeavor. Finally, Wheaton organized her high school alone, and Glen Ellyn students were sent there on a tuition basis. This did not meet the needs of the village; but for the time being, at least, the situation seemed to be satisfactory.

At right, the program from the first commencement. 1894, Glen Ellyn High School

1915 to 1919: Honeysuckle Hill and Biester

The first class of Glen Ellyn High School Graduates.
Classes met at the DuPage County Bank in 1916.
Mr. Holtzman was Glenbard High School's first principal.

When Wheaton raised the tuition rates in the fall of 1915, Glen Ellyn residents, through their grammar school board of education, established their own high school. The increased tuition rates may have been the result of some resentment of having Glen Ellyn students at the Wheaton school. State Superintendent of Education Francis Blair telephoned his department's recognition of the new school to County Superintendent R. T. Morgan on September 15. A portion of the DuPage County Bank Building was rented for classrooms and on Monday, October 4, over fifty scholars in the freshman and sophomore classes assembled there.

Two teachers Arthur M. Holtzman and Miss Erin McMechan, had been employed to supervise them. Mr. Holtzman was a graduate of North Central College at Naperville and had been teaching at a private school in Dundee.

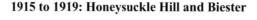

First class, Glen Ellyn High School, 1894

Once organized, the high school grew rapidly: first report cards - - with grades on a percentage basis - - were issued on November 12, and the new school's football team played its first game with Wheaton's second string on November 19. The result was a 20 - 6 defeat for Glen Ellyn.

At its organization, the Glen Ellyn High School offered a two-year course. It soon became apparent, however, that the grammar school board did not have the taxing power to finance the establishment of a complete, four-year high school. An election was held, and a separate board of education, consisting of Louis J. Thiele, president; Mrs. Ralph Treadway, secretary; and Mrs. Calvin Berger, Sidney Badger, B.E. Curtis, Dan Norman, and W. W. Reed organized the Glen Ellyn Township High School on December 27,1915. Under a 1911 act of the Illinois legislature, the high school could be placed on this basis, and the new board optimistically perfected plans for the future.

No class could graduate the first spring, but the board made arrangements for more classrooms during the summer of 1916 by adding a third floor to the bank building. The following September, seventeen members of the senior class who had been attending Wheaton High School began their last year in Glen Ellyn. This class, the first to be graduated, gave leadership to the school and initiated many extracurricular activities before they graduated. Their graduation was held in the high school's auditorium on June 7, 1917.

At this time, the faculty numbered five teachers and the principal.

The act, under which the high school was organized, was declared unconstitutional by the Illinois Supreme Court in November 1916. The situation thus arising left the school without legal backing, and many moments of anxiety followed. As over one hundred other schools in the state were similarly affected, the State Superintendent of Education advised the local authorities to continue operation of the school. A bill was passed by the State Legislature in early 1917, which gave the school the necessary legal foundation.

1915: A portion of the DuPage County Bank Building is rented for classrooms and on Monday, October 4, over fifty scholars in the freshman and sophomore classes assembled there. Two teachers Arthur M Holtzman and Miss Erin McMechan, are employed to supervise them. Pictured below, the students of Glen Ellyn Township High School, 1917.

As mentioned earlier, Louis J. Thiele served as president of the school board for years. Sadly, his name and efforts are largely forgotten. His name is just not the household name that Fred Biester enjoyed, but Mr. Thiele's service needs to be mentioned here. First of all, he served on the school board for decades. Not only was he instrumental in the genesis of Glenbard High School, but he also was the person who hired Fred L. Biester.

From Louis J. Thiele's obituary: He was born in Chicago, married 16 May 1899 to Miss Anna K. Houge, and came to Glen Ellyn to live in 1902. For a number of years, he was a salesman for Sprague Warner and company. Mr. Thiele was an outstanding citizen of Glen Ellyn. He was interested in establishing the early "Glen Ellyan" newspaper He directed the Glen Ellyn Orchestra at its first concert on December 1, 1912 and assisted the Glen Ellyn Musical club through its first season, 1913-14. Mr. Thiele started the high school Glee club and directed it in 1917-18. He was a member of the Mendelssohn club of Chicago. The first president of the high school board, which later became the Glenbard board., he continued in this position for 14 years. He was instrumental in formation of the Illinois State School Board Association, in starting health supervision in the village schools and hiring the first health nurse. Together with William H. Baethke, Mr. Thiele started a survey of the village for the formation of Grace Lutheran church in 1908. For years he directed the church choir. Mr. Thiele always supported betterment and beautification projects for Glen Ellyn during his long residence here.

World War I, Ousting First Principal, German Removed from the Curriculum

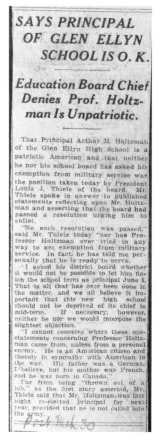

Louis Thiele also navigated an especially tenuous time in the early life of the high school. America entered World War I on April 2, 1917. In March of 1918, a signed petition was given to the school board demanding that the teaching of German be eliminated from the curriculum. The petition read:

"We the undersigned citizens of Glen Ellyn hereby petition you to discontinue at once the teaching of the German language in Glen Ellyn High School. The world is in a great fight for democracy. The evidence is overwhelming that the German government recognizes that the teaching of German in our schools is a great aid to its cause. Sworn testimony before the senate committee investigating the German-American alliance has been given by German born officers showing that they used their greatest efforts to have their language taught in our school to aid propaganda. Germany and German ideals stand for all that is abhorrent to a democratic people. Let our boys over there know that German propaganda is not encouraged in Glen Ellyn schools."

The school board acted on the petition, eliminating German from the curriculum. A German Club would not form at Glenbard West until 1962. What is not known is how Mr. Arthur Holtzman, Glen Ellyn High School's principal (pictured, right), became a lightning rod for controversy. Somehow, his German last name caused Glen Ellyn citizens to question his patriotism, urging his to prove his patriotism by joining the United States military. Citizens became incensed when they learned, erroneously, that school board requested a military exemption. In several back-and-forth newspaper articles, it was Louis Thiele who finally clarified that the school board did not request a military exemption for Holtzman, but a deferment should his draft number be called.

Incredibly, the March 30, 1918 Tribune printed an article that added to the tense situation. The article stated that not only did the school board eliminate German, but that Holzman was fired. The article even called Arthur Holzman "Prof. Fritz," a derogatory term for a German man.

In a letter to the Glen Ellyn papers (see photo, at left), Thiele explained that Holzman was perfectly willing to be called into service, but that the school board had asked that, should his number be called, please allow Holzman to finish out the school year.

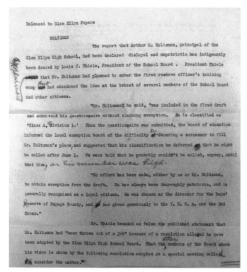

One interesting fact is that, while Arthur Holtzman was an American Citizen, he was born Canadian. His mother was French, and his father had immigrated to Canada from Germany.

It is unclear why, but Mr. Holtzman resigned in May 1918 to enter military service. Perhaps the patriotic crisis or anti-German sentiment ushered him out. Perhaps he was asked to resign. Neither of these are confirmed.

What is known is that he had given several years of diligent work to the community in the establishment of its high school, and he left his work to the regret of many of the villagers. Principal Holtzman suggested that the board select as his successor Mr. Fred L. Biester, with whom he had had contact in Y. M. C. A. work. The new principal, a native of Belvidere, Illinois, was a graduate of North Central College at Naperville. He had taught three years at Naperville and one at East Aurora. Mr. Biester came to the school in the fall of 1918. Arthur Holzman does come into the story one more time when he wrote a letter dated March 3, 1956.

charging her with the alienation of affections.

GERMAN BARRED FROM SCHOOLS OF GLEN ELLYN

No more German is to be taught in the schools of Glen Ellyn. This action was taken by the school board last night following a petition by citizens that the teaching of German be eliminated in the high school.

The ruling automatically removes from office Prof. Fritz Holtzman and at the same time nullifies its request that he be exempted from military service.

A resolution to the effect that the professor be requested to join the colors was adopted and will be forwarded to the exemption board today.

The petition was acted upon by President Louis J. Thiele of the school board and Trustees Sidney Badger, Mrs. Berger, Andrew Fox, and Superintendent Reed.

"The success of any venture is predicated on the loyalty of the individuals responsible. Today at Glenbard you have everything. In the fall of 1915 we had nothing, no student body, no curriculum, no building. But when the students who composed the first classes of Glen Ellyn High School assembled for their first meeting, they had what you can't find in books: a Team Sprit, and a great desire to have their own school, regardless of the obstacles, and there were many.

So I salute the first two graduating classes of Glen Ellyn High School, and their first Board of Education. They are the ones who made Glenbard possible.

My second salute goes to Fred Biester, a great Educational Administrator. Thirty-five years out of thirty-eight is a unique record. Never has a recommendation of mine turned out so well.

Yours very sincerely, Arthur M. Holtzman

In April of 1919, state authorities awarded the Glen Ellyn High School full accreditation; during the same month, the school's board of education considered purchasing a site for the new building. The board members realized that suitable locations of the size needed for the high school were fast disappearing, and one should be purchased while available. From among the other sites listed on the ballot, Honeysuckle Hill, was selected in the election in August of 1919 and about 25 acres were bought from Charles R. Raymond for $8,000. The land had a 500-foot frontage on Crescent Boulevard and included all of the hill and Lake Ellyn.

Glen Ellyn High School Best Friends the Subject of an A&E Film—Which Never Airs

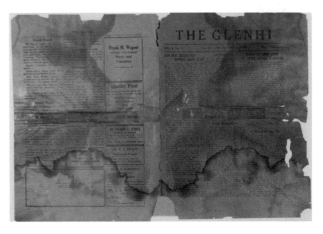

At left, the graduating class of Glen Ellyn High School. Glenbard High School was not officially named "Glenbard" until 1922. Also, notice that three of the graduates are Annie Bailey, Mildred Patch, and Helen Myers. The friendships they forged and kept became the subject of an A&E documentary. Julia Roberts was so touched by the story of their friendships that she narrated the show. Sadly, the documentary never aired—despite several attempts by the family and friends to contact A&E.

Below, a celebration of Annie Bailey's 100th birthday. All 25 of her great-grandchildren attended her party. This page was found in *The Grey Beard*, an alumni newsletter that is now, itself, retired.

The school received title to the property in November, the local newspaper reported on November 7, "On Wednesday afternoon a number of high school boys who volunteered for the job, began to chop down trees, and clear away the growth on the island." The lake was drained and preparations were made for the athletic field which was developed by filling the lake's south end. The organization of the Glen Ellyn Park District at the same time made possible the purchase of several acres of woodland surrounding the lake. Since the property had been unattended for several years, a matted undergrowth covered it. In 1923, the high school deeded the lake to the park board with the stipulation that it revert to the high school should it ever cease to be a lake.

Although the school board had raised sufficient money for the purchase of the hill property, funds did not exist to construct a suitable building. A move toward acquiring the necessary money was made in 1920, when the school board received $13,250 in delinquent tax receipts.

At right, *THE GLENHI*. The first issue of the high school newspaper. It is dated February 1919.

1920's: The Castle is Built

It was obvious that some other method of financing a high school building would have to be found, and the board explored the possibility of unification with a nearby town. Since Wheaton had its high school, the board turned toward Lombard. Seventy-five Lombard teenagers attended high school, some of them in Glen Ellyn, and parents were interested in providing facilities for them. At the request of the Lombard Parents-Teachers Association, several members of the board laid the suggestion plans before a meeting on February 16, 1921.

Among the points presented at the meeting, Lombard residents learned that the Honeysuckle Hill site was within one-half mile of the geographical center of the proposed district and their unification would enable the towns to establish a school as large as any in the county, with an attendance of about two hundred pupils.

At left, the man many consider the Father of Glenbard: Fred L. Biester. His influence was first felt in the fall of 1918 as the principal of Glenbard High School. He later became the superintendent of Glenbard High School District 87. Mr. Biester passed away on March 20, 1962, just months away from his retirement. His remarkable career touched parts of six decades.

In March several petitions, bearing the signatures of 645 Lombard voters and representing more than 75% of the village's voting population, were filed with the county superintendent of schools. The petitions requested direct annexation of Lombard to the Glen Ellyn High School District. Favorable action was taken on the petitions on April 9, and the election for members of the enlarged district's high school board was held April 16. The organization of the new board, on which residents of both communities served, followed immediately on April 25.

At a board meeting on January 1922, the petitions of district voters requesting an election on the erection of the building were presented. Subsequently, on February 11, two issues were decisively approved at an election in which 1,179 voters participated. One issue involved building the school, and the other, issuing bonds to pay for it.

When Lombard was annexed to the district, the board of education announced it would change the district's name in such a way to represent both communities. A contest was held among the students, and the name GLENBARD was suggested. By a resolution of the board, this was the district's official name after May 15, 1922. Construction work was started in the early spring and continued over the summer. By autumn, sufficient progress had been made that the cornerstone could be laid. The stone's laying occurred on September 10, 1922 and was preceded by a suitable program.

The building was designed to fit the location by Coolidge and Hodgson, (the successor of Shepley, Rutan, and Coolidge) the architects who also planned the administration building (at left, top) at St. Olaf College in Northfield, MN as well as Chicago's Art Institute (at left, below), Chicago's Public Library and building at the University of Chicago. Compare the architecture of those two buildings with Glenbard High School. The building was erected in the English Collegiate style of architecture, the walls of red brick with Bedford stone trim. One of its distinctive features was the leaded window panes set in stone. Below left, one of the last remaining leaded glass windows, taken from the 6th floor (Tower). The windows were replaced with Thermopane windows which greatly reduced the building's draftiness.

During the first few weeks of April 1923, the school's equipment was moved from the bank building to the new high school. First classes were held on April 19,1923, but the dedication was delayed until May 15, 1923.

Fred L. Biester's Letter Describing Building Construction Details

The following is from a document found in our archives in March 2019. It was part of a letter from John L. Biester, class of 1936, the son of Fred L. Biester. Attached to John's August 15, 1992 letter was the following from Fred L. Biester, date unknown.

The present High School Building is the result of four separate building project or units. The first, or west unit, was built in 1922-23 and contained facilities designed for not to exceed 600 students. Classrooms, gymnasium and heating plant were

some major provisions in the first unit. The central part of the building which comprises the tower, library and classrooms was erected in 1926. By 1931 the student body had outgrown the available facilities and the auditorium unit was added. This unit provided space for the commercial department, music, study hall and class rooms in addition to the auditorium. The building project just completed has for the most part been an expansion of available facilities which no longer provided adequate room for a student body of 1,140. It provides classrooms, study hall, shop, band room, household arts room and additional gymnasium space.

One of the difficult problems to be faced in the construction of a school building when it has to be built in several sections is that of having a unified building capable of efficient use and unity of appearance when it is completed. In these respects, the present High School Building now presents a beautiful appearance with little evidence of not being a single structure and with very few major handicaps so far as its use is concerned even though three different architects have had to be employed during the process of its construction.

The contour of the land upon which the Glenbard building has been built has presented no end of problems from the standpoint of adequate light inside of the building, proper elevations, proper approaches so far as entrances and exits are concerned, as well as a suitable type of architecture. The building has six floors, the tower having a fifth and sixth story. It has a total of fifteen outside entrances and exits, these being distributed on three different floor levels which means that you can walk out of the building onto the ground on three of the six story levels. The type of architecture is modified Gothic and certainly lends itself well to the setting in which the building has been placed. In fact, almost no one who sees the building for the first time has any other reaction than that it is one of the most beautifully located school plants in the country.

The building contains the following facilities: Thirty-six class rooms, three science laboratories, a library, two good size study halls, a student club room, gymnasium 95 x 100 with a seating capacity of about 1,300, girls' and boys' shower and locker rooms, an auditorium which will seat 1,600, a well-equipped stage, suitable dressing rooms, adequate offices for the administrative staff and the athletic directors, adequate first aid room, a fairly adequate amount of space allotted to the various shop courses and a cafeteria which can seat between 400 and 500 students at a time.

While this may appear to be a rather liberal amount of space, it must be remembered that including students, faculty and other help about 1,200 people must be taken care of inside this single building each day. The average college has four and five times as many buildings for a student body of half the size. All of the building is now assigned for service with the exception of two rooms. Of course, not all of the rooms in the building are being used up to capacity, facilities being adequate for an increase of 100 to 150 students.

Without question the young people have a building and campus of which any student body would have reason to be proud. The District, through the fine cooperation of its people, has an institutional plant which is among its finest and best assets.

The Controversy of Glenbard's Anniversary: 1916? 1922? 1923?

There is some discussion on the actual anniversary of Glenbard (Glenbard West) High School. Did it begin in 1916 when the high school program began in the bank? Or did it begin on May 15, 1922 when the school district officially become the Glenbard Township High School District?

At this point in time, the official start of Glenbard High School was Tuesday, May 15, 1923, due to that day's official dedication. As it is stated, above, "classes were held on April 19, 1923, but the dedication was delayed until **May 15, 1923.**

Also, the 75th anniversary celebration was held during the 1997-1998 school year. (See the 1998 Pinnacle yearbook.)

The 100th Anniversary celebration will be held during the 2022-2023 school year, with **Monday, May 15, 2023** as the 100th birthday of Glenbard (West) High School.

The Building is Completed

The portion of the building completed in 1923 was everything west of the tower, and it was designed for an enrollment of 400 students. The enrollment in November 1925 was 423, and Mr. Biester estimated it would be between 475 and 500 for the 1926-27 school year. The tower addition, added in 1926, included new offices, a library and a community room that would seat 150 persons. The tower itself contained a classroom for the head of the English department with a fireplace and bay window on the third floor, music room on and an art room on the fifth floor. The expanded building was occupied in September 1926 by 487 students.

Below, right, the graduating class of 1924 sits in front of the high school. The main entrance part of the building was not yet built. The trees, behind the students, would give way to the main entrance part of the building.

Above left, an early championship basketball team. Above right, the graduating class of 1924 sits in front of the high school. The main entrance part of the building was not yet built. The trees, behind the students, would give way to the main entrance part of the building. At the right, Glenbard's very first yearbook, 1934. On it, there is a signature of Marian Nebraske. Also, the mailing reads "Winston C Pray." Below, a page from

My Class Mates. Since the students did not receive a yearbook to collect signatures, they would bring in their own stationary and collect signatures. These pages contain no dates, but it is believed to be from the late 1920's or early 1930's.

At left, a rare, pre-1940 photo, courtesy of Ricardo Sharrardo. Posting it on Facebook, he wrote that this is a "1933 photo of Bobby Grieve. I came across this photo in my Great-Uncle's (Cyrus B. Stafford) photo album. He and Bobby were friends in school."

Also, while attending Glenbard High School, Bobby Grieve ran the 100-yard dash at 10 seconds flat in the 1932-1933 season. Compare that time with another 100-yard dash record holder, Harold "Red" Grange. A future football great, Grange ran the dash in the 1920-1921 season in 10 2/5 seconds. After Glenbard High School, Bobby Grieve ran track and played football at the University of Illinois. Enrollment continued to increase and by January 1930 the projected number of students for the 1931-32 year was 800. A new addition, which was dedicated February 8, 1931, was attached to the west side of the building.

The 1,558-seat auditorium with dressing rooms and a glee club room below the stage ran south toward Crescent Boulevard. The wing running north from the auditorium provided rooms for the Commercial Department, a band room, a cafeteria and four unfinished classrooms.

Glen Ellyn and Lombard continued to grow and by 1938 the facilities were too small. With assistance from the Public Works Administration the necessary funding became available and the construction work began. The gymnasium wing was expanded to the west and south.

This expansion provided facilities on the first floor for industrial education and music; science, physical education and student activities on the second; offices and a first aid room on the third; and classrooms on the fourth. In the northeast wing the four unfinished rooms were completed, and a new foods lab was built on the second floor. Part of the new space was available in the fall of 1939, and the work was completed in 1940.

At left, the 1922 Glen Ellyn Township High School basketball team. The school was not known as GLENBARD until May of 1922, indicating that this picture was taken during the early part of the 1921-1922 school year. At right, Fred L. Biester, Glenbard's first football coach.

Below and at left, two early football teams. Dates unknown.

An Undefeated Season

The 1926 Glenbard High School Football Champions

Back Row (Left to Right): Coach Streaky Burnett, Al Sjogren, George Johnson, Unknown, Unknown, Unknown, Bill Starrett, Coach Bud Butler

Middle Row (Left to Right): Tommy Gregg, Unknown, Phil Ganzhorn, Harry Surkamer, Ben Wold, Frank Gilbertson, Unknown, Paul Graves

Front Row (Left to Right): Sam Wilbur, Spenny Bond, Red Thompson, Zing Zearing, Bill Tillman, Scaldy Mallin, Unknown, Tiny Heiden, Hollis Cash

The yearbook, *The Pinnacle*, was not published until 1940 when English Department chairman, Henry J. Firley, wrote, organized, published, sold, and distributed the school annual.

THE POWERS THAT BE

GLENBARD'S BRAIN TRUST

Here are a few internal pages from the *Glenbard Yearbook 1934.*

According to the last page of the yearbook, the publication (editing and business management) was done by the Junior and Sophomore Journalists, composition was done by the typing classes.

The cover art was created by Dorothy Walker. Cartoons by Jack Entler. No faculty advisor name is given credit for the publication.

COUNCILS OF THE MIGHTY

SNAPPY SNAPS

At left, boys pile into a car in Circle Drive. (From the 1940 *Pinnacle.*)

The organization of a high school district and the construction of a building were important, but the educational activities they facilitated were more significant to the communities which were served. The course offerings for the 1919-1920 year were as follows: English (4 years), French (2 years), Latin (3 Years) algebra, geometry, advanced algebra, solid geometry, commercial arithmetic, physiography, physiology, penmanship, drawing, ancient-medieval history, modern history, American history, civics, economics, zoology, botany, physics, bookkeeping, commercial geography, stenography-typewriting (2 years) and physical training (2 years).

Below left, the graduating class of 1935. Glenbard's yearbook, *Pinnacle,* was not available until 1940. There was an attempt to publish a yearbook in 1939, but it fell short of the votes (students committed to purchasing the book) to print it. Instead of a yearbook, students would receive a class picture.

Below, the graduating class of 1936. It is one of the few photos that features Mr. Fred L. Biester standing with the class. He is in the front row, just to the right of center. At right, Fred L. Biester with his car in Glenbard's Circle Drive.

At left, the football team from the 1920's—most likely 1923, 1924, or 1925. The coach is Mr. Carl Palmer.

In the spring of 1924 the school was evaluated, and accepted as a member, by the North Central Association of Colleges and Secondary Schools. The daily time

schedule consisted of eight, 40-minute periods and one section of 20 minutes, but in 1927 the administration decided to change it to provide time for supervised study to better meet the requirements of most colleges. The new schedule consisted of One, 16-minute section and seven 55-minute class periods.

In the first three decades of its existence, Glenbard High School became well known in the state and the nation for its leadership in education. Along the way there have been a few occurrences of other kinds by which the school came to the attention of the public.

One such occurrence was the filming of "Along Came Jack" by the Atlas Educational Film Company in the fall of 1925. According to local newspaper articles, several students and local adults had "starring" roles. Parts of the film were made at a Glenbard football game, a local home, and a local church.

The instrumental music program was started in 1926. The Conn School of Music offered one lesson per week at a cost of $3.50 per month.

Right, the Chicago Office of the Atlas Educational Film Co. It was located at 29 Madison St. The movie, "Along Came Jack" was filmed at the high school. As of the printing of this book, no copies or further information about that movie is available.

1920's and 1930's: Classes and Clubs

Through the cooperation of the Chicago Motor Club and the Illinois State Highway Department, a five-week course in sportsmanlike driving was offered to a limited number of juniors and seniors in the fall of 1938. A dual-control car was used in the driving course for the first time during the second semester of the 1938-1937 school year.

A council of residents sponsored adult night classes in the fall of 1937. The course offerings were: Spanish, French, English, English literature, sociology, amateur photography, and Spanish guitar. Teachers for this program were furnished by the Public Works Administration in 1938. Student activities were a part of the School program from the first opening for classes. Among the earliest were the athletic teams.

At right, the 1931 basketball team.

At left, the 1937-38 basketball squad

The boys' athletic program was very successful and won the following championships: basketball in 1925, 26, 34, 40 and 44; Cross country in 1927, 33, 35; and football in 1926, 27, 28, 27, 31, 34 and 37; and outdoor track in 1927, 33 and 35. The Girls Athletic Club was formed with 10 members in the spring of 1926.

At left, student artwork. The GWHS Historic Society found it, loose, in a drawer filled with other papers. The signature reads, "olson." It is not known if it was an art project, an idea for a yearbook cover, or a club coat of arms.

Two early student organizations were the Hi-Y club for boys, and the Girls Reserve. The first student council meeting was held On October 10, 1924. During that same year the Latin Club was formed, and the first homecoming dance was held after the York game on December 19th. The Glen Bard, the successor to the Glen Hi, received its charter from the national honorary journalism society, "Quill and Scroll" in the fall of 1928.

There was an active Science Club and in 1929 the members constructed a television set on which pictures could be seen by looking through a one-inch square hole. In 1932 the National Thespian Honor Society accepted the Glenbard drama group for membership.

Above are two samples of the graduating class pictures which were given to the seniors. The yearbook, *Pinnacle*, did not begin until 1940. Until that time, seniors were given these pictures to remember their class. Classmates then passed around paper or autograph books to collect names and messages. As of this printing, the GWHS History Society is **missing** the years 1917, 1919, 1920, 1925, 1932, 1933, 1934, 1936, 1937, and 1938.

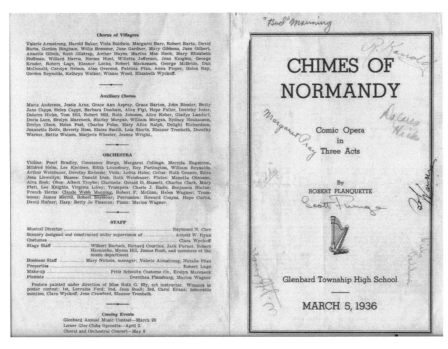

ANNUAL OPERETTA

Friday, March 15th

RESERVED SEAT
Fifty Cents

Sect.......... Row.......... Seat ....

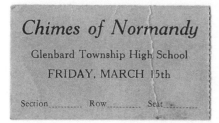

Chimes of Normandy

Glenbard Township High School

FRIDAY, MARCH 15th

Section.............. Row.............. Seat ....

At left, a picture from an unknown date or production. Circa 1930's.

According to 1969 GWHS graduate Russ Ward and shared via Facebook, February 2018:

"The top picture is the stage in the Glenbard Auditorium in April of 1935. The play was called Joan of the Nancy Lee, a comic opera in the style of Gilbert and Sullivan that apparently had something to do with pirates. The girl in back on the left is Miss Helen Wagoner, my Mom. And the following year, Glenbard put on an outstanding musical comedy production of Chimes of Normandy. These shows are what gave my Mom the bug to go on with her singing career. Lots of Glen Ellyn names in the program.

My brother graduated in 1964 and our mother in 1936. Her older sister, Lois Wagoner was in the first graduating class to use the new auditorium for their ceremony. In fact, I knew a lady who graduated from Glenbard when it was still located in the bank building on the NW corner of Main and Crescent."

Glenbard High School used to put on annual operettas. Pictures courtesy of 1969 GWHS graduate Russ Ward. His mother was Helen Wagoner.

1940's: Glenbard High School and World War II

Senior Class

GEORGE SEYFER, Vice-President
JOHN MALM, President
ALLAN WESSEL, Secretary-Treasurer

There were no yearbooks (*Pinnacle*) until 1940. Before 1940, graduating seniors would receive a class photo. An attempt was made in 1939 for a Pinnacle publication, but Fred Biester cancelled the printing due to lack of students being able to commit to its purchase. This is not surprising since the country was still in the grip of The Great Depression. The first Pinnacle finally arrived in 1940, under the faculty leadership of English Department Chairman Henry J. Firley, shown right.

Below, top, the first library. It was located where the deans' office currently stands. Above, a photo taken from the 1940 yearbook. This was the original gymnasium.

Below, bottom, after Biester Gymnasium was added in 1958, it was known as the Girls' Gym or the Hilltop Gym. The animals in the picture must have been part of a donkey basketball game. 1947 graduate, Harold "Snub" Pritchard reports that Fred Biester was a fierce competitor.

At left, the 1940 Glenbard High School basketball team.

Cliff Peterson, the captain, holds the ball.

The coach was Mr. Kietzman.

On Monday, December 8, 1941, principal Biester assembled the student body to listen to F.D.R.'s famous "Day of Infamy" or "Pearl Harbor" speech before Congress.

World War II affected the Glenbard Community in much the same way it did hundreds of others across the United States. Many graduates and some of the students were among the first to become members of the military forces.

The students continued to come to school go to class participate in the activities and in some instances, go to war. As much as the school tried to continue the normal routine, the war had an effect on all those who were involved with the "Castle on the Hill." There were meatless menus at the school cafeteria, the use of school buses was curtailed because of gasoline and tire rationing, and volunteers were urged to drive athletic teams to games and meets. Even the curriculum was modified to include basic aeronautics, physical activity that included a military-type obstacle course and instruction in restyling used clothing. The students purchased war stamps and worked in Community activities such as Red Cross and bond drives.

Finally, the war ended and Glenbard renewed its efforts to develop a strong educational program and an outstanding facility.

Below, the posters made by Glenbard art students to support the war effort.

At left, a 48-star flag donated to the school by teacher C. A. R. Johnson. Mr. Johnson, pictured left, served in the U. S. Naval Reserves. He took a leave of absence from teaching to serve during World War II. The flag was flown over the reserves in San Diego, California, as well as displayed in his classroom.

Above, left, the 1944 West Suburban Championship basketball team. Above, right, the basketball team from the late 1940's or early 1950's. It was found, loose, among a shoe box of photos. Written on the locker room wall is a quote by Teddy Roosevelt, "The only man who never makes a mistake is the man who never does anything." Notice that the photo is very normal—very traditional, with two exceptions: In the front row is a player (#11) without a shoe. Next to him is a player (#13) without a shoe or sock.

The First Students of Color

We (the GWHS Historic Society) believe that the Mitchell brothers was the first African-American student to attend all four years and graduate from Glenbard High School. Elliott Mitchell (left) graduated in 1947 and his brother, Edgar Mitchell (right) graduated in 1949. He later became a principal at a school in Vancouver, Washington. Pictured, right, is Edgar Mitchell on the Glenbard Track Team.

The period following World War II was one of unequaled growth in the school population of Glenbard. The building of new homes within the boundaries Of District 87 seemed to increase each year at an exponential rate. It was also a time when more students aspired to a college education. It was estimated that 63% of the girls and 88% of the boys in the Class of 1947 planned to attend college after graduation. That year, over 75 colleges and universities sent a representative to the College Night program.

1950's: Post-War Growth and Glenbard East

ROSAMOND DuJARDIN

By the 1949-50 school year, the enrollment was 1,206 and three new teachers were added to the faculty. This was the year the Pep Club was organized and started sponsoring student buses to out-of-town games; Henry J. Firley, English Department Chairman, won - the Midwestern Writers' Poetry Prize for his poem "Sundown and Dawn Together"; and Rosamund DuJardin, a local author, used Glenbard and Glen Ellyn as the background for her book Practically Seventeen.

During this time, the DuPage Tuberculosis Association sponsored a project to provide a free chest x-ray for all Glenbardians.

Donations from class treasuries, students, and the community paid for the World War II Memorial plaque (right) and it was dedicated in November 1949.

The Class of 1923, the first class to graduate from the Castle, had their reunion and homecoming in the fall of the 1950-51 year. It was Glenbard's first Homecoming. *The Glen Bard* reported that a donkey basketball game was held and Principal Fred Biester was the last faculty member to remain on his donkey.

At right, Nancy Jeanne St. Pierre's "Spirit Hat." It is believed that the hat was either a homemade product or was part of a class project. According to 1969 graduate, Glenn Reynolds, the hat was worn by freshman. They had to wear it in the building—especially around upper classmen.

The faculty numbered 61 during the 1953-54 year, and the Glen Bard under the leadership of Miss Helen McConnell, pictured left, first received an award for superiority among high school newspapers in the nation.

At the start of the 1952-53 year the enrollment was 1,368 and Mr. David Miller (right) had joined the staff as administrative assistant to Mr. Biester.

Here are the 71 Names on the WWII plaque near the main entrance. It is unknown to us, the GWHS Historic Society, what the "EX" means before some of the years.

The plaque reads as follows:

In honored memory of these men of Glenbard High School
who made the supreme sacrifice in World War II

1. John Allison 1939
2. Lawrence H. Anderson EX-1934
3. Owen Baer 1939
4. Robert Becker EX-1941
5. Edward Biehl EX-1941
6. William Black EX-1941
7. Emery Boardman EX-1938
8. Melvin F. Bohnhoff EX-1940
9. Ralph Carlson 1934
10. Donald Chiles 1939
11. Donald Dettmer EX-1937
12. Robert T. Duncan 1936
13. John Fargo 1934
14. Herbert Feist EX-1935
15. Alden E. Ford 1941
16. William H. Furner 1937
17. Stuart W Gathman EX-1934
18. Herbert S. Gilbert 1934
19. Forest Gimlin 1927
20. Vernon L. Gray 1940
21. William Grieve 1939
22. Joseph G. Hancock 1939
23. William Helm 1938
24. John Herboth 1930
25. Carlton Hibbard 1934
26. Richard Hitzeman EX-1937
27. Harvey G. Hoganson 1942
28. Arthur L. Johnston 1938
29. Einar Julian 1939
30. Don F. Julien 1936
31. Carl E. Kant 1942
32. Robert R. Kimbell 1930
33. Ralph L. Knippen 1942
34. Alvin W. Koehn EX-1944
35. Thomas W. Kopper EX-1937
36. Jack C. Kreamer 1931
37. John Kreitzer EX-1941
38. Lawrence M. Lehne 1941
39. Ted Lindholm 1938
40. Robert W. McClure 1942
41. Lee McPartland 1936
42. Robert E. Mason 1943
43. Frank L. Mead 1934
44. Frank C. Miller 1943
45. James E. Milmoe 1933
46. Frank L Moulton 1944
47. Lyle G. Moyer 1942
48. Jack Mueller EX-1938
49. Raymond Mueller 1943
50. Roland Nelson 1940
51. Daniel O'Malley 1935
52. Arthur Fred Otis 1943
53. Ramon Patheal 1941
54. Donald Pieri 1938
55. William D. Rogers 1938
56. Charles Russell 1937
57. Edward Sample EX-1942
58. Everett Satzke EX-1942
59. Arthur J. Smith 1939
60. Morton E. Smith 1937
61. Warren Smith 1933
62. Roy Soldman EX-1940
63. Cyrus B. Stafford 1933
64. Jack Stauffer 1931
65. Roman T. Stelmore 1941
66. Howard Thompson 1927
67. Raymond Tuhey EX-1937
68. Martin Weimer EX-1942
69. Arthur H. Weinbauer 1940
70. Richard T. Wilson 1943
71. Omer Yocum 1943

At left, the 1952 addition. The stairs begin on Crescent Blvd. The photo is dated 11-28-52.

It also reads, "Clarence Jensen – Architect A. L. Jackson Co. –Builders

At left, the class trip to Washington D. C. in 1952. It is uncertain when these began and who went or even when they ended, but the class trips to Washington seem to have been an annual event.

1954-55 was pretty typical year for the athletic teams. In the West Suburban Conference, the football team won 0, lost 7, and tied 0; the Cross-Country team won the Conference title; the basketball team had 18 wins and 7 losses (and won the DeKalb tournament); and the baseball team won 18 and lost 7.

At left, the football from the Homecoming football game. It was tradition to have the players sign it and give it to the homecoming queen, Bette Carlson. On this particular football, one of the players also included his phone number. The date reads October 15, 1971 from the Class of 1972.

At the start of the 1955-56 year the enrollment was 1,853. There were 67 faculty members and Driver Education was instituted as a regular course. In November 1955 a supporting shot was fired in the battle to relieve the very crowded conditions at Glenbard when a group of Lombard residents presented the Board of Education with a request for the establishment of a second high school to be located in Lombard. The academic facilities were stretched to the breaking point and the physical education and athletic facilities were so inadequate that the physical education program did not meet the mandate of the state.

In March 1956, the state courts decided that the area of Bloomingdale which had petitioned to leave the Glenbard District would remain in District 87. On May 26, 1956, after many months of promotion by the school administration, the voters of the district approved a bond issue to build Glenbard East and a new gym at the Glen Ellyn campus.

This was also the first year the Senior Washington, D.C. trip travelled by airplane instead of by train. There was one other item of interest in the 1955-54 Pinnacle. On page 100 under Senior Royalty, "The Pinnacle staff thanks Fran Allison and Burr Tillstrom of Kukla, Fran, and Ollie for selecting the 1956 King, Queen and Court." (pictured right)

1956-57 was another year of crowded classrooms and corridors, and inadequate physical education facilities. Some relief seemed to be on the horizon as construction on a new gym was started.

At left, two students relax outside the high school. The photographer was Dave Menard. He wrote to Dr. Thorsen (2006-2013) that stated, "I was lucky enough to have attended Glenbard from 1950-54. I cannot recall who the two students are in the photo, but I think the girl is Midge Smith, '54." (Pictured, right, Midge Smith's senior portrait, 1954 Pinnacle.)

The architectural rendering of Biester Gymnasium. When classes started in September 1958 with over 2,400 enrolled students, the gym was ready for use, including classrooms in space that was to be used as dressing rooms in the future. On December 7, 1958, the new gym was dedicated to Fred L. Biester in recognition of his service to the youth of the community. This rendering was "lost" until the spring of 2017 when Adrian Villanueva, our maintenance foreman, found it.

Work on the Lombard school was underway and even with some serious construction delays plans were being made to open at least part of the building in the Fall of 1957. In July 1957, Mr. Fred L. Biester was formally appointed superintendent of District #87 and when school started in September, Glenbard Township High School became Glenbard West High School with Mr. David H. Miller as Principal.

Glenbard East High School opened with only Freshman and Sophomore students, and Mr. William E. Rider as Principal. (Picture taken from the Pinnacle when Mr. Rider served as Dean of Students at Glenbard West High School.)

With the new gym and over 500 students at Glenbard East, crowding was eased for all aspects of the program. The athletic coaching staff looked forward to being able to build a stronger program that would allow more students to participate.

First Homecoming, Torchlight Parade, Pep Rally and Bonfire: October 6, 1950

Glenbard's very first Homecoming Pep Rally was held on Friday, October 6, 1950. According to the 1951 Pinnacle, "Student Council's most outstanding contribution was to work with the new Glenbard Boosters' Club this fall to sponsor the Hilltoppers' first Homecoming."

According to The Glen Ellyn News, "approximately 1,500 people gathered for the pre-game pep rally which followed the torchlight parade Friday night." Jane Karr (pictured, left) was crowned queen, making Jane Karr the very first Homecoming Queen in Glenbard's history. The next day, on Saturday, October 7, 1950, Glenbard lost to LaGrange on a "wet and dreary day." The final score was 26-6.

In 1952 the student members of the Hi-Y club built the fire. At right, the 1955 bonfire.

According to the 1940 Pinnacle yearbook, "The Hi-Y Club, a boys' organization, is the high school branch of the YMCA. Any boy who agrees to live up to the platform of clean living, clean athletics, and clean scholarship may join the club. The purpose of the club is to 'create, maintain, and extend throughout the school and community high standards of Christian Character."

A 1970 Glenbard West grad, Mark Luginbill wrote, the tradition of the bonfire "began in 1952 and continued annually into the 70's. It was then stopped for a number of years due to concerns that the bonfire was adding to air pollution. Happily, common sense has prevailed, and the bonfire is an annual event. Also, back in my day and dating back at least a decade, we had the torchlight parade. The torches were soup cans stuffed with balls of newspaper that had been soaked in kerosene nailed to a 3-foot stick. After the homecoming pep rally at Biester, we lit the torches, marched around the lake and encircled the wood pile and threw the torches onto the pile starting the bonfire. Remarkably, this was all done, to the best of my recollection, without faculty/firemen supervision." At left, a receipt for 5 gallons of kerosene used to light the torches for the parade that led to the bonfire.

Luginbill continued, "One of my best memories is that in the second semester 1970 I was head of the Grounds Committee which was responsible for picking up litter on the campus as well as policing the parking lot. For a reason I don't remember, my role merited a building key which among other things opened up the door to the tower. So, on nice days, after I made my round of the campus, I would grab my lunch and eat it out on the tower." As a member of the Grounds Committee, it was his purchase of 15 gallons of kerosene that helped illuminate the parade.

Due to the horrific 1958 fire at Our Lady of Angels (Catholic elementary school, shown at right), Glenbard High School was soon required to remove all wooden floors. According to several faculty members (now retired), during one of the summers when Dr. Elliott was principal (1972-1987), seniors who had been hired to remove the floors asked where they should take the maple planks. "Chuck them over by the lake," the principal said. In the fall, the homecoming pep rally burned the old floors in that year's Homecoming Bonfire.

To this day, seniors who build the fire are known as Woodchucks. To be a Woodchuck, students are required to apply for the honor.

AP Photo/File

The day of the bonfire, students are excused from class as they stack the wood. Each one receives a special Woodchuck t-shirt, pictured at left and modeled by class of 2019 graduate, Katie Sinta.

1960's: Glenbard High School Becomes Glenbard West; The passing of Fred L. Biester

1960-61 was a time to build on the frenzy of the recent past and get used to the idea that there were now two Glenbards. The Cross-Country team won the State Championship again. 1961-62 started with a new principal, Mr. John D. Sheahan, at the helm.

At the district level, Mr. Biester had indicated he planned to retire in the near future, and he started the search for a new superintendent.

On March 20, 1962 Mr. Biester died, just 3 months from his retirement. The entire community was shocked. Fred L. Biester had been a part of Glenbard for 44 years.

At right, one of two portraits of Fred L. Biester. This portrait currently hangs in room 428, The Alumni Room.

At the right, Fred Biester's "This I Believe" essay is cast in bronze and hangs next to his portrait in the Elliott Library.

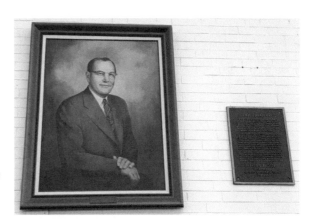

My whole living is based on an unchangeable faith that I have been created as a part of an eternal plan. I know very little about the plan, and my contribution will be infinitely small, but it is important as each drop of water that makes an ocean.
I believe God has such a purpose for each individual and that my greatest contribution to successful living is to believe that every individual has something fine and great in his personality and that I have an obligation to help everyone I contact to realize all that is fine and great within him.

I believe I can reach my own best self by a profound, compelling faith in God and a conscious effort to think more often about the welfare of others than of my own satisfaction.

Fred L. Biester
Superintendent
Glenbard Township High Schools 1918 – 1962

The Board of Education appointed Mr. Sheahan, Principal of Glenbard West, to be the interim superintendent and proceeded to hire Dr. Dean W. Stoakes who Mr. Biester had chosen to be the new superintendent. Dr. Stoakes officially became superintendent on June 11, 1962.

An era in the development of public education in the community, county and state had come to an end and the mantle of leadership was passed to new individuals.

The leadership For District #87 was different for the 1962-63 school year, but the problems were not. The number of students enrolled increased and it was apparent that there were new space needs. Not only was there a need for general classrooms, but some specialized facilities were outdated and inadequate for the number of students enrolling in the courses that required these facilities. Curriculum and teaching methods in the sciences and foreign languages were in desperate need of improvement. Biology, physics, and chemistry labs built in the 1920s were designed for a lecture-demonstration teaching style.

Modern teaching methods called for students to have hands-on experiences in order to understand how a scientific principle is developed rather than read about it in the textbook and see a demonstration prepared by the teacher. Foreign languages were being taught as courses with almost all the emphasis on the reading and writing of the language. Among the many

changes in teaching styles in foreign languages was an emphasis on being able to speak the language. Language labs where students could listen to tapes of persons speaking the language and also respond in the language were essential to implementing this teaching method. These kinds of curriculum improvements and modern teaching methods required more space. There was talk of double shifts. After an unsuccessful attempt in November 1962, a referendum in March 1963 to raise the education tax fund rate and for a bond issue were both approved by the voters.

1963-64 was another year of construction for the students and faculty at Glenbard West. Plans called for an addition to the building at the end of the wing running north from the auditorium lobby, remodeling of the cafeteria, moving the home economics foods lab, conversion of the speech classroom under the auditorium stage to dressing rooms and a few other changes. The addition would contain an instrumental music room on the first level and a choral room on the second level. At right, the main entrance as it appeared in1960.

Both levels would have individual and small group practice rooms and an office for the instructor. The third and fourth levels were devoted to physics chemistry and general science labs. Both levels had adjoining labs separated by a folding partition to facilitate team teaching. Students and teachers had to adjust to changing conditions as the work progressed. As in past years disrupted with construction, students did learn, and extracurricular activities were successful despite the inconveniences.

Pictured: 1961 Prom. King Pete Birch and Queen Nanci Jones

The Silver Anniversary of the *Pinnacle* was one indication that this was true.

When school opened for the 1964-65 year the addition and remodeling work was complete, and the new facilities were scheduled for use. In addition, electronic lab equipment had been installed in one of the foreign language classrooms over the summer. The new foods lab allowed the Home Economics department to offer Boys' Chef for the first time, and it proved to be a very popular course. Early in the year, the student body voted to change the Student Council to the Students' League. The main thrust of the change was to reach each student and in so doing to involve more students in school activities.

Glenbard Football and Athletics Gain the Glenbard "G" –and a New School Color

Although the Varsity football team had a losing streak at the beginning of the season there were signs of hope for the future of the program; four of the players were named to the All-Conference team and the head coach, Mr. William Duchon, was voted DuPage County Coach of the Year. As coach of the Hilltopper football team, his record was 93-44-3. He passed away in 2017.

Glenbard West's school colors have always been green and white. And yet, the color we currently known as "Glenbard Green" was not the original Glenbard Green!

According to former Athletic Director Blaise Blasko, originally "Glenbard Green" fell somewhere in between the dark Forest green and the brighter, Kelly green. This made athletic uniforms costly, due to the constant upcharge for the custom color. It is believed that the change happened in the early 1970's. According to the Glenbard Township High School District 87 Identity and Styles Guidelines, the new and correct color of Glenbard Green is Pantone 626.

New Glenbard Green

PANTONE Opaque Couché
Pantone 626 C

Original Glenbard Green

Kelly Green

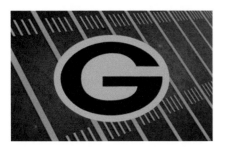

Additionally, Coach Duchon is credited with creating the Glenbard "G," borrowing the design from the Green Bay Packers. On the left is the Glenbard "G" used by Glenbard North High School. Below, the official "G" of the Green Bay Packers. Finally, Coach Duchon also created the Hitters' Club. These football players were allowed to wear special helmets spray painted gold. For more about the Hitters' Club, see the special chapter on Bruce Capel, the Original Hitter. The Glenbard School District 87 school board named the football field after Bill Duchon in May 1981.

The years 1965-66 and 1966-67 were characterized by a Glenbard Township High School a degree of normalcy because there was a minimum of outside influences such as construction. The addition of Russian to the Foreign Language course offerings in 1965-66 was one sign of the work being done to update the curriculum. Increasing student enrollment continued to strain the existing facilities.

A bond issue was approved by the voters of the district and ground was broken in August 1966 for the construction of Glenbard North High School in Carol Stream. Everyone knew that things were going too smoothly and were wondering what the next disruption would be. The disruption was Mother Nature.

Pictured at left, on January 27, 1967, there was a record snowfall in the Chicago area, and for the first-time classes were called off at Glenbard West for one day.

In order to accommodate the large enrollment, both Glenbard East and Glenbard West implemented an over lapping class schedule for the 1967-68 school year.

On Sunday January 7, 1968, a water line for the sprinkler system in room 426 broke. Fortunately, a teacher had entered the building and discovered the water running down the stairs from the fourth floor. The water had damaged rooms 426, 217, 218 and 217, and the Principal's offices on the 300 floor. The custodial staff, and a group of teachers and administrators managed to get the water shut off and the damaged areas cleaned up, so they could be used on Monday morning.

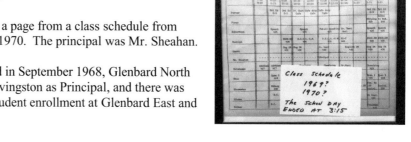

At right, a page from a class schedule from 1969 or 1970. The principal was Mr. Sheahan.

When school started in September 1968, Glenbard North opened with Ray Livingston as Principal, and there was some relief in the student enrollment at Glenbard East and Glenbard West.

On the athletic front, the 1967-68 golf team won the West Suburban Conference title; the 1968-69 Varsity football team won the conference title for the first time in 29 years, and the baseball team won the conference title for the third time since 1962.

By the end of the decade, the dress policy had relaxed. English teacher, Virginia Gannon (pictured at left) is credited as the first female Glenbard teacher to wear a pant suit.

In the 1968-1969 school year, the Glenbard varsity football team became the first football team in school history to have an unbeaten record—with no tied games.

1970's: Glenbard West and Unrest

Pictured at left, a signed poster by the 1970 Chicago Cubs. As a benefit, the Cubs played the Glenbard West faculty. Signatures include Baseball Hall of Famers Billy Williams and Ron Santo. During the 1970's, Glenbard West felt the impact of unrest related to many of the national problems, most prominent of which was the war in Vietnam.

1967-70 started with a degree of uneasiness on the part of the school administration. Things were happening outside the control of the school that would have great influence on all aspects of life within the "Halls of Ivy".

It all came to a head on May 8, 1970 when about 100 students refused to go to their assign classes and assembled on the lawn in front of the school to protest the actions of the National Guard at Kent State University. (See photo on next page.) Unfortunately, it was also the day a Career Fair for all Glenbard District students was being held in Biester Gym and West students had the opportunity to go to the Fair during non-class time.

The Principal and the Dean of Students met with the student protesters, and the faculty was advised to take extra care to protect the students for whom in they were responsible and to be extremely accurate in their attendance. records for each class. The school administrators (pictured at left) were very concerned that some sort of confrontation might occur between the protesting students and other students - or even with persons not a part of the school. The local police were notified of the situation and were requested to be available, but to not enter the school grounds unless specifically requested to do so by the Principal. Around noon the students returned to their classes and the protest ended peacefully.

The protest was really only the beginning. In the days that followed some parents questioned the Principal's actions in carrying out his responsibilities to the State of Illinois and the Board of Education for student attendance. A few expressed their view that he should "look the other way" and allow the students to decide if they should attend classes. Others were very disturbed that the US Army had been allowed to have a booth at the Career Fair to present information about military careers. And, of course, there were many rumors and half-truths that had to be explained to the students and the community.

It was a time of contradictions. There was pressure to allow students wide choices in how each one would accumulate the total number of credits to graduate. Almost every academic requirement was questioned, and some students refused academic honors, and yet the "It's Academic Team" was a popular extra-curricular activity. Relevance became the litmus test for any changes in the curriculum. All rules became suspect and the prevailing attitude was "rules are made to be broken" - or at least constantly revised to justify positions that will be popular. This was a time of serious problems such as drugs being sold inside the building and frivolous questions such as, "How short is too short for the length of a girl's skirt?" or "Should male teachers be allowed to have a beard?"

Many policies were revised and new ones instituted to allow students to express themselves freely and to hear representatives speak to all sides of an issue. One of the new procedures delineated the steps to be taken to arrange for after school use of school facilities to debate questions of importance to any group of students. The procedure was only used a few times because very few students were interested in staying after classes to participate either as speaker or a part of the audience. When properly handled and coordinated with existing curriculum, many of the changes produced better education. However, change for the sake of change produced little. There was also pressure to have a more ethnically and racially diverse staff. There were some who wanted to put such considerations above experience and academic preparation. The administration tried very hard to find qualified candidates who would bring diversity into the classroom.

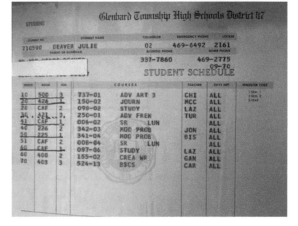

At right, Julie Deaver's class schedule. Julie graduated in 1971.

The changes that characterized Glenbard West in the 1970's and 1980's were far-reaching and greatly accelerated by the events of that time. The instructional program, which had not grown and developed during the unrest of the 1960's, was strengthened and expanded; financial concerns became a constant challenge as the number of students increased and a changing technology demanded newer hardware; the autonomy and self-determination of the building was diluted by a larger and more intrusive Central Office staff; and the role of parents and students became pervasive.

In the midst of all of this change emerged Radio Glenbard, known by the call letters WGHS. This was a short-range FM station. It went "On the Air" for the first time to serve the students and residents of the Glenbard West attendance area.

Enrollment climbed to nearly 2,400 students until, with the opening of Glenbard South, it began a slow decline to about 1,700 students. Finally, nearly 50 teachers on a veteran faculty that had been hired primarily by Fred L. Biester, and who had added so much to the reputation of the school, were retired. By the spring of 1987 the turn-over from the 1971 faculty was over 85%. They were replaced by newer and younger teachers who had new ideas, attitudes, and approaches to their profession but who were as effective as their predecessors. Both "faculties" made Glenbard West synonymous with excellence.

When Principal John D. Sheahan announced his retirement in 1971, Dr. Robert D. Elliott, Assistant Superintendent at Oak Park-River Forest High School was appointed his successor. (See photo, right, Dr. Elliott's portrait that now hangs in the Elliott Library.)

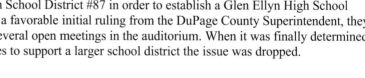

Because of contractual problems Elliott did not begin his duties until January of 1972 and William Dutch, Assistant Superintendent, served as acting Principal.

The District faced a $1,000,000 deficit when voters rejected an increase in the Educational Fund and budget cuts of $650,000 were made in several critical areas. Freshmen were limited to four classes, the reading specialist and the social worker were eliminated, class size was increased, supply budgets were slashed, and the number of coaches was reduced.

Another immediate concern for the new administration was the daily schedule. Because of overcrowding the school had been on an overlapping shift. There were no study halls or homerooms and students were free to leave the building or campus if they had no assigned class. The 1972-73 schedule added an eighth (tutorial) period, required study halls for first- and second-year students, and assigned Freshmen to homerooms.

A third concern was the presence of an active group in Glen Ellyn who sought to remove Glenbard West from School District #87 in order to establish a Glen Ellyn High School District - Receiving a favorable initial ruling from the DuPage County Superintendent, they proceeded to hold several open meetings in the auditorium. When it was finally determined that Glen Ellyn lacked the necessary financial resources to support a larger school district the issue was dropped.

Design by student Tia Rush

By the end of 1975, the financial picture was even darker and the District had a deficit of nearly $4,000,000. Additional and more extensive budget cuts were necessary. First and second year students were limited to four classes unless there was as opening in an existing Class after the sixth day of attendance, but tighter controls on class size and the elimination of classes with marginal enrollment made such openings unlikely. Even with the reality of a larger enrollment, the number of teachers was reduced; Supply budgets were cut again; and, for the first time, students had - to pay for summer school. Teachers returned to school without a contract and the word "strike" was heard more frequently.

To make matters worse, the voters had defeated by 54 votes a bond issue to enlarge the facilities at Glenbard North. A second vote in January 1976, approved the proposal so that North could eventually accommodate 3,000 students.

The release in February of a study by the Citizens Facility Committee created more uncertainty when it suggested "that perhaps the time has come to close one of the buildings." West seemed to be the logical choice because of its age and operational costs. After a very heated and emotional response to this idea from the Glen Ellyn Community the study was quietly shelved.

Attempts to strengthen the academic program in the face of budget cuts were not helped by the negative actions of a vocal minority who were continuing to protest movements of the 60's and our continued involvement in Vietnam.

Pictured, student Tia Rush, the winner of a GWHS logo contest. A 1972 contest to design a school flag was won by Tia Rush, class of 1973, from among 50 entries. Tia joined the faculty in 1978.

The first issue of the Glen Bard in 1973 complained that Glenbard lacked a free press; demanded a smoking area; and cited "increasing restrictive school policies" on daily attendance, tighter hall restrictions and library conduct, and controls on the distribution of materials in the building.

The refusal of distribution rights for misleading information on the effects of LSD was, somehow, connected with the pardon of Richard Nixon. When an outside underground newspaper, "The Conch," was denied the right to distribute their paper in the building, the matter was heard by the Student Council Court of Appeals (their first and last case) and the decision of the Principal was upheld. The office of the State Superintendent later reversed that decision.

The first Senior Honor Convocation was held, successfully, amid predictions that some students would try to disrupt it. A committee of teachers established Criteria for the Senior Honor Medal which was awarded to Bette Carlson at the 1972 Commencement.

In the next two years, plans for an outdoor graduation were rained out and the idea was dropped until 1983. The first leadership conference was held for West students and became the forerunner of the District Leadership Conference. An early version of the Citizens Advisory Council was begun in 1974 with a group of parents meeting with the Principal to discuss school problems and concerns. To give parents an opportunity to visit classes in session, a series of six parent visitation days were set up in 1973.

An honors convocation for Freshmen was begun in 1975. Bill Kurtis a well-known Chicago television anchorman, pictured at left, was the guest speaker.

Perhaps it was the approach of the Bicentennial, but with the opening of school in 1975 there was a new and refreshing attitude toward school and toward life. More interest and pride in achievement, a search for positive values, and a nearly visible spirit permeated the halls and classrooms. The only cloud on the horizon was the "Holy War" brought by the discontent of a group called "The Glen Ellyn Nine."

The controversy began when a minister inquired about the presence on campus of some religious groups, prayers by the football team, and the use of the public-address system for announcements by outside groups. Ten ministers requested that the Board of Education "continue to develop a policy regarding the conduct of religious activities in district schools. " It was the opinion of the Principal that some of their concerns were valid and, with other building administrators, who had not escaped similar charges, some practices were revised and tightened after approval by the school attorneys. The Glen Ellyn Clergy Council indicated its desire to "disengage itself" from any further controversy.

The matter was thought to be closed when a well-known Chicago clergyman wrote an inflammatory article in a national magazine, creating an instant market for local and national media. Reaction on both sides was immediate, strong, and often indiscriminate. A religious controversy tends to provoke nonreligious conduct. The Glen Ellyn Clergy Council was split, members of opposing Churches bickered and Glenbard West was accused by some of furthering the controversy because so many faculty and staff were members of one particular church. The Board of Education had little choice but to formulate six official policies dealing with religious issues. One cannot escape the conclusion that the petty jealousies between churches was played out in the public forum of the school.

When Superintendent, Dr. Dean Stoakes, announced his retirement in early 1977, the Board of Education named his assistant, Ray Livingston, (pictured, left) as interim superintendent. Their announcement in December that Mr. Livingston would not be considered for the permanent position infuriated the faculty and community. At a mass meeting in the West Auditorium, dozens of speakers voiced their strong support of Mr. Livingston and their displeasure with the way the matter had been handled by the Board of Education. In the face of so much genuine support the Board reversed itself and awarded him the position. The Livingston Award is still given to this day in his honor. Faculty members are encouraged to nominate students who exhibit the five qualities. The nomination form reads as follows:

The following items are examples of behavior that would merit a human relations award. They are not intended to be exclusive or complete. A Livingston Human Relations Award could be presented to a student who:

1. Exhibits courage in defending the rights of others.
2. Befriends others regardless of socio-economic, racial, religious, ethnic or academic background – discourages the formation of "cliques."
3. Shows consistent kindness and courtesy to staff and to other students.
4. Performs sustained volunteer work within school or community.
5. Exhibits cooperative spirit consistently with students and staff in classrooms and co-curricular activities.

The Instructional Program

Glenbard West had long been recognized as an academically sound school and its students added greater luster and substance to that reputation in the next twenty years. In spite of more stringent graduation requirements, the disconcerting effects of budget cuts, attendance boundaries and student unrest they continued to achieve and excel in all areas of school life.

Left, students push a VW Bug down Crescent Blvd.

The final report of the North Central Evaluation Committee in 1976 noted that, "Glenbard West is a very, very fine high School. It is a school that has an enviable teacher-student relationship and rapport. West has an outstanding educational atmosphere which is business-liked and relaxed without being casual. It has a distinctive personality and character."

At about the same time, the Principal, Dr. Elliott, was named as one of 60 principals in the country to participate in a Study on "effective schools", an honor that belonged to the entire school. A year later, the Chicago Tribune named Glenbard West as one of the ten outstanding schools in the Chicagoland area. The faculty and students were cited for ". . . the dramatic appearance of the school . . . student loyalty and pride . . . and a standard of excellence developed in more than half a century. " Glenbard West's heritage, tradition and discipline were also mentioned.

During this period Glenbard West strove to improve the quality of instruction and to broaden the curriculum. There was a need for more Honors and Advanced Placement Courses to challenge the better students, and more attention needed for lower ability students. In 1972 there were honors sections only in English I and English II, the other 16 courses were one-semester offerings. There were no honors sections in foreign language and only two each in mathematics, social studies, and science. A Humanities course, team taught by English social studies and art teachers was introduced and met on Tuesday and Thursday evenings. A third year of Honors English was added.

1980's: Computers, a Vietnam Memorial, a Movie, and a TV Show

Part of the reason for the lack of progress was the dilution of academic standards at all levels of education, one of the of the results of the massive doubt and unrest that characterized the 1960's. Another reason was the limitations of the community to support their schools. Budget cuts do not promote academic progress. Each building was responsible for instruction and curriculum development with the result that similar courses in different buildings varied greatly in title, content, and objectives.

There was little coordination between buildings. It was not until 1980 that the District took the initiative in standardizing and evaluating courses and in establishing uniform Course objectives. The number of Honors and Advanced Placement courses increased, and a program adopted for gifted students. The numerical value of some grades in Honors sections was increased. There were now three years of Honors English, and one year of Advanced Placement. Foreign Language had two years of Honors sections in all languages, and Advanced Placement in two languages. Mathematics and science offered Honors sections in three courses and Advanced Placement in two others. Social studies had three Honors courses and one in Advanced Placement. This progress was not without its critics, especially from those who did not qualify for higher level courses. They reasoned that too much time and money was spent on those who least needed it. It was felt that inflation of Honors grades gave the average student less chance to compete for a higher GPA, and that there was less effort to develop courses and sections commensurate with the abilities and interests of low average and basic students. As the school population changed with the admission in 1982 of students from Glenside Junior High School, Glenbard West received more students with special academic needs, needs which some felt were not being met. In 1989, nearly a third of Glenbard West students came from Glenside Junior High School.

The increasing involvement of the District improved the quality of instruction, but also accelerated the movement toward Centralization of authority and decision-making and reduced the autonomy of the building and its staff. While this is an inevitable consequence of a larger and stronger central office staff, it, nevertheless, represents a permanent change from past practice. The program of computer use and instruction began in 1979 with 13 computers in one room. Pictured right, from the 1983 Pinnacle.

By 1985, it had grown to occupy five rooms when Glenbard West was selected by AT&T to be a demonstration Center for "Writer's Workbench", the first Computer based program to analyze Student writing. The computer evaluated grammar, word usage, spelling, etc. and provided a printout for teacher and student use.   As the only high school selected for this new technology, Glenbard West benefitted greatly from the large number of visitors who exchanged ideas with the staff, and from the latest equipment which AT&T made available to the students and staff.

An enduring contribution to the community occurred in 1983 when the students and faculty honored the 13 Glenbard West Students who died in the Korean and Vietnam wars. A bronze tablet honoring the dead of World War II was a fixture in the front lobby when James Benfield (class of 1961) suggested that a similar recognition be given to those who had died in Asia. His suggestion was approved, and a committee was convened to formulate plans for an appropriate memorial.

Art teacher, Mr. DeVaud, (pictured on the left) designed the eagle and made the clay model of the bronze tablet, and a Chicago Firm completed the tablet at a cost of nearly $1,500, all of which was paid by contributions from students, school groups, and local donors. It seemed fitting that this memorial to the sacrifice of one generation of Glenbard West students be sponsored by a later generation of students. An overflow Memorial Day crowd was present when Seniors Linda Pals and Kian Lloyd presented the tablet to Mr. Wallace Capel, whose son, Bruce, was an early Vietnam casualty. It was a moving tribute to those whose service has been so often questioned and attacked. One mother wrote: "After all these years they are no longer the objects of ridicule and hatred." For those who were present it was, perhaps, the start of the healing process. It reads as follows:

IN HONORED MEMORY OF
THESE MEN OF
GLENBARD WEST HIGH SCHOOL
WHO MADE THE SUPREME SACRIFICE
DURING THE WARS IN
KOREA AND VIETNAM

RICHARD LEE BLASEN '65	EDWARD LEE GUSTAFSON '66
DIETER HANS BURGER '58	RONALD EDWIN HAGSTROM '66
JOHN BRUCE CAPEL '61	RONALD LEE HOUDEK '47
WILLIAM WALTER DICKEY '51	ROBERT FRANCIS MORGAN '56
THOMAS BENEDICT DUFFY '64	RICHARD PHILIP ROBBLEY '59
JAMES RICHARD FOLEY '56	CRAIG BRIAN SCHIELE '61
	JOHN FELLOWS SCULL, JR. '64

DONATED BY THE GLENBARD COMMUNITY

The following is the script for the 4-minute YouTube video: "Bruce Capel The Original Hitter."

This story shows how one man, even in his death, can set an example for always trying your hardest. Bruce Capel had a short life, but one lived with such values that even now, 52 years later, his life has become both legend--and lesson.

His name is John Bruce Capel, but everyone called him Bruce. A graduate of Glenbard West High School in Glen Ellyn, Illinois, Bruce was everyone's favorite. Tall, handsome, kind, and thoughtful, Bruce was also the star player on the football team. He could play so well and hit so hard that the coach would call him "The Hitter." His number was 50.

After graduating from high school, Bruce played football for the University of Illinois where he played with Dick Butkus. Together, they won the Rose Bowl. But Bruce couldn't keep number 50 because Butkus already claimed it, so Bruce took the next number up, 51. This is important, because Chicago still honors number 51, as you will learn in a moment.

It was after college that Bruce went into the Marine Corps where he played football. But Bruce told the Marines that he didn't join the Corps to play football. He wanted to serve his country. You can guess the rest of the story. He was shipped out to Vietnam where, shortly after his arrival, his platooned was ambushed and killed.

Before he lost his life, Bruce had taken the time to write a letter to a 6-year-old boy from back home. (See Jack R. Griffin's column, "This Marine Took Time to Care" reprinted, with permission, on the next page.) Pictured at right, 6-year-old Steve Edelson.

Bruce's fiancée, a gym teacher named Melodee Galik, had noticed that one boy in her class, Steve Edelson, cared more about sports than academics. She asked Bruce to write Steve a letter about the importance of always doing your best and trying your hardest. That letter was found on Bruce's body--written, but not yet sent. Steve's story and the letter were published in the Chicago Sun-Times, May 26, 1966.

Bruce's death was a hard loss for his family, fiancée, the community, and for his former teammate and roommate, Dick Butkus. Once Butkus was drafted for the Chicago Bears, he took Bruce's number, 51, to honor him and his life. Butkus' career was so impressive that, not only did he make it into the Football Hall of Fame, but the Chicago Bears even retired #51--the number worn by Dick Butkus--and his friend, Bruce Capel.

To this day, the football players at Glenbard West High School are called, collectively, The Hitters, to honor the way that Bruce played football and lived his life--always trying your hardest.

So what happened to that 6-year-old boy, Steve Edelson? The boy his father is quoted in the newspaper as saying, "I am sure that Steven will look back on this letter in the years to come and, hopefully, part of Bruce's feeling for his fellow men will show itself in my son."

It turns out that Steve Edelson took Bruce's advice, doing his best in everything he did, creating a - highly-successful company, buying several minor league sports teams, and serving on the Board of Governors for Hebrew University and a Trustee at the Truman Institute for Peace.

Said Edelson in a 2018 telephone interview, "There's a formative time in your life when something like that (getting the letter from a soldier) happens and it becomes a big deal. You think about it a little more. Here this fellow is in Vietnam leading people as he did on the football field--the consequences are substantially different, but thanks to his fiancée's caring, he was in the middle of a war and took time to write me a letter that I only got when somebody found it on his body when he was dead. You need to embrace every opportunity and pick up as many other people as you can."

Bruce Capel gave his life for his country, but his sacrifice went beyond the abstract concept of freedom and service. His sacrifice and his example became embedded into the lives of people like Dick Butkus, Steve Edelson, as well as those football players now called "The Hitters" and every student at Glenbard West High School.

Pictured, right, is author Steve Wiersum with Steve Edelson at the 2018 Distinguished Alumni Award ceremony. Bruce Capel was named in the of the first round of Distinguished Alumni awards.

The following is a February 2018 Facebook message from Laura Capel Claassen, the niece of Bruce Capel. It is reprinted here with her permission.

The Cvengros', neighbors across the street, were asked by my grandparents to please help see to it that the flag was flown daily in honor of Bruce. One day, the Cvengros' happened to look out their front window to see a bulldozer (driven by the builder) coming at the flagpole to remove it. They ran across the street to explain why it needed to stay.

The builder later returned to cut it down and stashed it alongside his own house that was next door to the Capel house. A local architect was in the process of buying the Capel house when all of this was happening and was distraught that the flagpole was gone, knew it had a unique finial that my grandfather specifically selected (USMC symbol of Eagle, Anchor, Globe), so years later when the builder moved away a sweet elder couple bought his house, noticed the flagpole resting beside their garage and noted the finial which told them it had special meaning. They decided to be its steward and wait to see if anything ever presented itself, wasn't causing any harm where it was.

Two years ago, the architect was cutting through their yard because he sold the Capel house to a young family with five kids and it was then that his eyes caught sight of the eagle to the finial peeking out from under a pile of leaves. He dug down and was shocked to uncover it.

He then called the Cvengros' son, Andy, to let him know. Andy visited the stewardly neighbors and the neighbors said he could have it back but not until they cleaned it up properly first.

After they heard Andy explain the story about Bruce, they laid sheets down, cleaned the flagpole while shedding some tears. Andy, a former Hitter himself and gold helmet recipient from Coach Duchon, and another Hitter placed an extension back on the flagpole to return it to its original height.

At that point in time, Glen Ellyn was building a Veterans Memorial and so the flagpole accepted its new duty to again fly the American flag in its new location, near the field where Coach and Bruce loved to be. An interesting side note about Andy and the flagpole. Andy remembers like yesterday, being five years old and playing cowboys and Indians.

He chose my grandparent's little memorial garden with the flagpole as his stake out spot. The kids were making a commotion and when my grandmother saw this little boy in her sacred place, she came out and initially started to scold him but regrouped, sat him down on the little bench and explained to him why that area was special to her.

Andy remembers looking way up and seeing the flag and finial. It's a memory that has stayed with him.

Ray Livingston Retires, Dr. Robert Stevens takes Distict 87 Helm

When Ray Livingston announced his retirement for June of 1984, Dr. Robert Stevens, Superintendent of the North Scott School District in Eldridge, Iowa, was named as Glenbard's fourth superintendent.

The year of 1983 saw other significant changes with the first outdoor graduation and a recognition of all graduates who had earned a 5.0 grade point average. The Senior Honor Convocation, which had been held during the regular school day, was held in the evening for the first time. In 1986, a change in its format made it possible for local scholarship donors to personally present their awards, the total value of which had grown to nearly $40,000. The next year letters for high academic performance were awarded for the first time.

The increasing clamor for greater accountability, and the quest for more tangible proof of learning, made the Illinois School Report Card almost inevitable.

Proponents of the 1985 School Reform Legislation wanted a statistical indication of how well each school was performing so comparisons and ratings could be made. The first Report Cards were mailed to parents in the fall of 1986. It contained college test scores, state and national averages, attendance and graduation rates, financial status, salaries, etc. Glenbard West came out extremely well on this report card, ranking in the top ten schools in the state.

Hollywood comes to Glenbard West: The Filming of *Lucas*

Glenbard West's debut into the world of film began when officials from 20th Century Fox approached the Principal with the idea of shooting a full-length film at the school. They were attracted initially, by the beauty of the campus, but they were persuaded by the attitude of the faculty and students.

As it turns out, *Lucas* came very close to not being filmed at Glenbard West at all. According to Dr. Elliott's daughter, Jeanne Elliott Enright, there were problems with the script. Dr. Elliott thought that it contained inappropriate language and situations. After some debate and deliberation, the producer of the film, David Seltzer, agreed. Seltzer rewrote the script so that Dr. Elliott would approve of having the film associated with the high school. Seltzer's daughter also made an appearance in the film.

Pictured, left, Dr. Elliott walks the set of *Lucas,* a 1986 American teen tragicomedy film directed by David Seltzer and starring Corey Haim, Kerri Green, Charlie Sheen and Courtney Thorne-Smith. The film was Winona Ryder's screen debut.

After approval by the Board of Education, shooting for Lucas began in June 1985, and continued through the summer and into December. Pictured, right, Steve Dahl and Garry Meier bring their radio show to Glenbard West during the *Lucas* filming. Several GWHS teachers were featured in the movie, including football coach, Jim Covert, pictured below. Coach Covert helped the actors run football plays.

Pictured, left, volunteers who appeared as extras received a *Lucas* t-shirt.

The movie grossed over $8 million. It was a unique experience to observe the intense effort, and the tedium, of film making, and to see the students, faculty, and parents captured in film. Also, the final movie had some changes from the script, but the only reshooting was the very ending-- not the hospital scene where Maggie gets Lucas to promise never to play football again.

The original ending had Lucas and the rest of the characters "we've grown to know and love" singing in a choir. Apparently, preview audiences actually threw things at the screen at the end because they didn't feel Lucas achieved a big enough victory for doing what he did. The new ending in which he finds a Park High jacket in his locker was done to answer that complaint. If you look at the movie, you can see that Lucas is noticeably older in the hallway locker scene than he is in the hospital scene. And his friend Ben has grown a lot between the hospital waiting room scene and the new hallway footage. The ending was re-filmed in February. Snow had to be removed and dried with heaters. Students entering the building were told to hold their breath, so it did not look cold.

An interesting stipulation that Dr. Elliott imposed was that the film would have its international premier in Glen Ellyn. Thanks to Dr. Elliott, *Lucas* premiered in March 1986 at the Glen Theater, complete with Klieg lights, tuxedos, limousines, and extensive media coverage on Glen Ellyn's new cable tv station. Pictured, at left, original tickets to the movie's premier.

Pictured, right, Charlie Sheen (Cappie) and Cory Haim (Lucas).

Tour de Glenbard Begins: 1985

The Tour de Glenbard begins in 1985, modeled after the Tour de France. Cyclists raced on a course that outlined the campus. It was sponsored by G.A.A—Glenbard Athletic Association. The original G.A.A. stood for Girls Athletic Association.

By 1988, Glenbard District 87 faced a budget deficit of nearly 10 million dollars. The cost of teaching a larger school population and the costs of building maintenance had escalated dramatically since the last rate increase in 1968. The prospects for a successful vote were not bright. In 1972, the voters had defeated a similar proposal to increase the building fund rate and had approved the addition to Glenbard North only after first defeating it.

In addition, there arose an active group of irate taxpayers who vigorously opposed any tax increase, and the District was requesting an additional 66 cents per $100 of assessed valuation from a community where only 25% of the residents had children in school. Surprisingly, the issue passed by a comfortable margin. The vote was the greatest possible vote of confidence in the students and teachers of the Glenbard high schools, and to their record of achievement. Perhaps the most visible indicator of excellence was their performance in the National Merit Scholarship Program. In the period from 1972-1987, 183 Seniors were named as semi-finalists, 149 of these became Finalists and 68 were scholarship winners. Another 325 were named as Commended Students. Annually about 18% of the Senior Class qualified as Illinois State Scholars. In 1985, Laurie Fields was named a Presidential Scholar, one of 141 so recognized nationally.

In the fall of 1988, Dr. Elliott announced his retirement for June of 1987, and was replaced by Mrs. Susan Bridge. A 20-year veteran of the system, Mrs. Bridge began as an English teacher at Glenbard East, served as English Chairman at Glenbard South, and came to West in 1986 as an Assistant Principal for Instruction. She served as Glenbard West's principal until 1995, earning her doctorate degree for her work on the history of Glenbard District 87. Mrs. Bridge is then addressed as Dr. Susan J. Bridge.

During her tenure as principal, MTV shot Yearbook at the high school, homes, and area of Glenbard West. Yearbook was one of the earliest experiments in "Reality TV" and it featured Glenbard West students as they experienced the joys and heartaches of their senior year in high school.

The pictures, below, are screenshots of the TV show.

THE WHITE HOUSE
WASHINGTON

October 9, 1990

To the Class of 1940,
    Glenbard High School:

I am delighted to send greetings to all those
gathered to commemorate the 50th anniversary
of your graduation.

The years go by all too quickly, so a gathering
such as yours is a wonderful opportunity to
renew ties and to relive those magic moments in
our past that are very dear to us now. Barbara
and I hope that you will derive much pleasure
from your reunion and from reminiscing about the
"good old days."

You have our best wishes for a wonderful
celebration.

George Bush

THE WHITE HOUSE
WASHINGTON

Santa Barbara

August 25, 1987

To the Class of 1937, Glenbard Township
    High School:

On the occasion of your 50th reunion, I am
pleased to extend my warm greetings.

I know that this occasion brings fond memories
and renewed friendships. Coming together in
this way, you honor your community, your school
and your fellow graduates. You also reaffirm the
American tradition of fellowship and goodwill.

Nancy joins me in offering our best wishes for a
happy celebration. God bless you.

Ronald Reagan

Glenbard also holds two letters from a sitting President to a Glenbard Class reunion. One is from Ronald Regan. The other is from George H. W. Bush. Both letters send warm wished to alumni at their reunions.

Glenbard West 1983-84   A Story of Success

Athletics and Activities

The Hilltoppers compiled an outstanding record in the West Suburban Conference in the 1970s and 1980s. The boys won 30 titles in nine sports and the girls won 16 titles in five sports. Considering that Glenbard West was usually the smallest school, and did not compete in swimming, badminton, or soccer (until 1977), it is an impressive record.

The football team won 13 titles, including seven straight title from 1971 to 1977. They finished second in 5-A competition in1976 and won the title in 1983.

Glenbard West enjoyed championships seasons in golf (7), wrestling (3), indoor track (2), and Cross Country, soccer, basketball, baseball, and outdoor track. The Cross-Country team finished second in the state in 1972 and 4th in 1975.

In the early 1970's there were no interscholastic teams for girls. The sudden rise of athletic competition for girls, aided in no small degree by Title IX legislation, finally gave the girls their share of the facilities, dollars, and publicity that had long been reserved for the boys. Their rapid growth, however, spelled the end of a highly successful G. A. A. program. The only sport for girls in 1971 was tennis. Gymnastics, and track were added in 1972, basketball in 1973, softball in 1977, cross country in 1978 and soccer in 1984.

Pictured: Ginny Stein in 1973, the first year Glenbard West offered gymnastics. "I kept falling off the beam! I wasn't very good," Stein said, "but I had a lot of fun!"

Title IX and Glenbard West High School

Author's note: Sue Pariseau taught PE and math at GWHS for 35 years. During that time, she coached track for 29 years and cross country for 27 years.   The following is her account of Title IX, its impact on the athletic program at Glenbard West, and the opportunities it opened for female Hilltoppers.

By Sue Pariseau

Female athletes of today are far more physically fit and mentally stronger than when the girls' program started in the 1970's. Today, female athletes are highly competitive, and some are rewarded for their efforts with college scholarships. It's wonderful to see how the programs have developed to be able to produce the athletes of today Interscholastic sports for girls became a reality at Glenbard West after the passing of Title IX in 1972.

Title IX required any athletic program to offer girls the same opportunity as boys to compete in sports.

At Glenbard West, if you were teaching physical education, you were "recruited" to coach one of the sports that were being offered. Our athletic department was careful not to offer too many sports, initially. The thought behind that was to be sure that there was an interest in a particular sport and that the programs added would succeed. Surveys were handed out in gym classes to determine what sports would be added.

Girl's tennis had already been an established program and the interest for other sports seemed to be in Basketball, coached by Mary Lou Steiner, Gymnastics coached by Jane Leggett and Track and Field coached by Eleanor Arlen. The following year, Lynn Larsen became the Gymnastics coach and Sue Pariseau became the Track coach.

There were plenty of growing pains, as practice space became an issue. GAA, an intramural sports program for girls, had gym space before any athletic team could use the "Girl's Gym" which was located where Elliot Library is currently. There was no Field House, just Biester Gym with one main gymnasium and a 110-yard track downstairs. In the middle of the track was the wrestling area and in the SE corner a very, very small weight room.

The facilities were overflowing and needless to say, there was more than one "discussion" about who gets the practice facility first. The Athletic Department did an adequate job when it came to scheduling the facilities. Of course, no one was 100% happy, but it was fair for all. Eventually, maybe 3 years later, the GAA program dissolved due to lack of participation and that opened up more practice space for both boys and girls.

Shortly after basketball, gymnastics and track became established, volleyball was added. And then, after running on the boys' team for a few years, in 1978, the girls' cross-country team was officially added. As interest in girls' sports expanded, so did the number of sports available for girls to compete.

With boys' sports there were four levels: Freshman, Sophomore, Junior Varsity and Varsity. However, the girls' programs only had 2 levels, Junior Varsity and Varsity. This was true throughout the West Suburban Conference. It was several years later that the programs changed to F/S, JV and Varsity. The athletic directors, in an effort to develop strong, healthy programs made sure each sport could support two levels before adding a F/S level. The men and women who made up the conference athletic directors ensured that programs thrived.

One of the biggest obstacles to hurdle was finding qualified coaches who were willing to put in the time to make a program successful. There weren't many women who had experience in competitive athletics, as there had been no opportunities for women to compete, until now. There were different schools of thought when it came to male coaches. Some men saw working with the girls' programs, as an opportunity while others wanted no part of developing these programs. It took a good 10-15 years before young female athletes became coaches. Today, former athletes are coaching at all levels across the state, some at their alma mater, some in the same conference, some even at the college level!

A second major hurdle was educating the parents of the young girls who were participating in sports about the time and commitment necessary to become successful athletes. Today, girls are committed to their sport, attending practices daily, working off-season and managing their lives to become the best that they can be. It took time for the girls and their parents to move from and intramural philosophy to one of doing all that is necessary to become a competitive athlete.

And the last obstacle was helping the men who had been coaching in the WSC for many years to learn to share practice facilities, competition gyms, fields and weight rooms.

There was a lot of support for the girls' programs at West. The basketball team was very successful under the guidance of Emily Mollett and Jim Corso. Volleyball flourished with Steve Burkhart leading them to state championships twice and cross country, coached by Sue Pariseau, brought home a 3rd place and 2nd place trophy in state cross country meets. Today, all the girls' athletic programs are strong, healthy programs. Some athletes have even come back to be head coaches at their Alma Mater, Kristi Faulkner, Basketball and Christy Junta, Volleyball.

Female athletes of today are far more physically fit and mentally stronger than when the girls' program started in the 70's. Today, female athletes are highly competitive, and some are rewarded for their efforts with college scholarships. It's wonderful to see how the programs have developed to be able to produce the athletes of today.

This generation of student athletes, boys and girls, have grown up with competitive sports as part of their daily life. Many don't realize there was a time when girls weren't able to compete! Thanks to Title IX, some wonderful administrators and the men and women who volunteered to coach, sports for girls are alive and well at Glenbard West High School.

No Room for PE Classes and More Sports Success

At one point in the 1970's, girls didn't take P.E. their senior year. The reason? The simple fact that the school didn't have the physical room to hold P.E. for Freshman, Sophomore, Junior and Senior Girls' P.E. The exception: Senior boys had to take their P.E. class.

The girls' teams won titles in track (5), basketball (6), volleyball (3), cross country, and softball. The volleyball team finished third in the state in 1981, came in second the following year, and were State Champions in 1983. The Cross-Country team finished third in the state in 1980 and second in 1981. During the 1981-82 school year, the girls competed in seven sports and won four titles.

Glenbard West has had several individual state champions. Todd Kuoni on the still rings and Steve Roskam in the all-around won gymnastics titles in 1982. Bill Fritz von the mile in 1973 and in 1974. Tom Stacey was the pole vault champion in 1981, Jim Cramton won the 400 meter in 1985, and Greg Blanchard the low hurdles in 1982.

GWHS Cheerleaders Featured in TV Commercial

In the 1973-74 school year, ten of Glenbard's cheerleaders became "overnight stars" when they made a television commercial for Rejoice Shampoo through the Leo Burnett Advertising Agency.

Varsity cheerleaders Karen Houdek, Peggy McKay, Kathy Reinert, and Paula Shanks, and sophomores Judy Biocca, Gail Healy, Shan Logan, Mary Jo Neville, Sophia Page, and Pam Sokol were chosen to go to Palatine where they each had one side of their hair washed with a leading shampoo and the other side washed with Rejoice. Six of the ten girls on the ad that was aired once in Milwaukee, said that the Rejoice side was softer.

At left, 1973-1974 Varsity Cheerleaders. Above, Sophomore cheerleaders.

The most unusual state champion, however, was Bridget Bowman who won six medals in swimming--a sport that Glenbard West did not have. As a Freshman in 1985, Bridget won the 500-yard freestyle in record time and placed third in the individual medley.

The next year she again won the 500-yard freestyle and set a record in winning the individual medley. In 1987, she broke her record in winning the 500-yard freestyle, won the individual medley, and was named Girl Swimmer of the Year in Illinois. The faculty also earned recognition in swimming when the school nurse, Jane Hill, set a national record for her age group in the 500 freestyle, and won the 50-yard freestyle. Pictured: Bridget Bowman and Brooke Bowman, who placed in the State Swimming meet. Bridget was an Olympic hopeful in 1988.

When the Suburban League was disbanded in 1974, Proviso East and Oak Park-River Forest High Schools joined the West Suburban Conference. Initial concern over Glenbard West's ability to compete with such large schools was soon dispelled, but the loss of the traditional game with Wheaton Central High School was a disappointment. The membership of the conference was altered again in 1984 when it merged with the Des Plaines Valley League to form a Gold and a Silver Division. The Old West Suburban Conference became the Silver Division.

Success in inter scholastic competition was not limited to athletics. The Forensics team won the Regional Title in 1986 and Joel Jeske (right) became Glenbard West's first state Champion in Winning Original Comedy. The next year Kristen Yarema won the title in Extemporaneous Speaking and repeated her success a year later when the team finished third in the state. Win Anderson made it four in a row when he won the Original Comedy event in 1989.

Opportunities for- titles are less common in Music and Drama but Glenbard West continued to excel in both areas. The band won several citations and the choir entertained thousands at performances in the community and at its two major concerts. The dramatics program consistently staged productions of high educational and entertainment value.

Glenbard West's publications, too, were a source of pride--even when their content made some uncomfortable. *The Glen Bard* won 20 Gallup Awards (17 in 18 years); the highest and most prestigious scholastic award for publications, many Quill and Scroll awards, and dozens of citations from the *Suburban Press*. Its writers and editors have been recognized frequently for their excellence. The paper has carried, often articles of depth and substance on issues outside the life of the high school. The hostage crisis, draft and amnesty, drug use, abortion, suicide, and environmental concerns were typical of their range of interest. (Pictured left, members of the *Glen Bard* staff from the 1966 yearbook.)

The *Pinnacle* has portrayed with accuracy and feeling the events of a school year, capturing in picture and print the human story of life in the "Castle." It is a publication which becomes more valuable with each year.

Byzantium, the student literary magazine began in 1981, grew into a vehicle to feature the best writing of a talented student body. It was later replaced by Archive when its format changed to an online, internet publication.

Over the years following its inception in 1967, WGHS, Radio Glenbard provided a valuable service to the School Community. However, student interest in the hard job of operating such a highly technical activity fluctuated from year to year, and the cost of maintaining the equipment was high. Because of Federal Communication Commission regulations, the station was going to have to make major and expensive changes in the equipment. As a result, the WGHS activity officially ended in June 1987.

More about WGHS, Glenbard West's FM radio station.

According to Stephen Reiger (Class of 1981), "Those were special times. It's funny: I acquired a broadcast reel to reel player (Revox A77- the same model we used in the main studio) and it's all refurbished and ready to go. I was just getting ready to play my air checks from back then.

I was technical director and on-air personality at WGHS while a student. One tidbit of information about WGHS and its difficulty in recruiting was that the station had an educational license from the FCC. Somewhere someone got the misconception that an educational license meant that the station had to dedicate a percentage of airtime to playing educational material. This ranged from in current events updates to my personal favorite (heavy sarcasm) The Adventures of Ookpick

The Artic Owl produced by the United Nations and arriving weekly in little blue boxes much to the derision of the station pledges (usually freshman) who wanted to be on the air in one of the very limited time slots. Turnover was high.

The station was only in the air after school until the custodian locked the school at 10pm. I can remember many a boring hour watching the tape reel moving through the machine while suckling my will to live as the UN droned on and on about

something or other. It was Gifford Gaynor (G squared we called him) that as station manager called the FCC to clarify the whole educational license thing up. It turned out that educational in the license meant that the license was granted to an educational institution for the training of radio personnel. Well happy days! We became the Rock of Glenbard overnight (not that we didn't play popular music later in the day)! It was a real WKRP moment when I ripped the stupid educational stuff off the tape machine (and threw it out the window- the trees near the station always seemed to be sporting reel to reel tape) and fired up the Rock N Roll. Getting rid of the dull programming really boosted interest. We even played music though the PA system during registration in August.

Pictured, left, Stephen Reiger

Yes, we were reprimanded for that on more than one occasion. The music publishing companies would send demos. We gave them airplay and asked for audience call in to put the track into rotation or dump it. If the vote was to dump it the record went out the window. That ended when we realized that the voting was turning to always dumping with people outside ready to catch the record. During my broadcasts I put a microphone out the window and left it on but at a low level throughout the entire broadcast. Some interesting messages were shouted into the mic over the years (or some students would ring the bell) although much was not intelligible since it was at a low level under the other program material."

The Castle Needs Repairs

With its striking architecture and its setting on the hill overlooking Lake Ellyn, Glenbard West is one of the most attractive high school campuses in the nation. If any building can be loved by its inhabitants, it would be "The Castle on the Hill." It, therefore, merits special mention in the history of the school.
To those who occupy the building for any length of time, however, it often exhibits a malevolent personality. After climbing the steep Honeysuckle Hill to get to the building, there were times when teachers, staff, and students were often greeted with leaking roofs, falling ceilings, extremes in temperature, and bees.

The Glenbard West teachers were rarely surprised or flustered by any unusual event; they learned endurance, fortitude and patience. During the late 1960's the District spent over $2,000,000 in plumbing, electrical work, and heating, much of which remained unnoticed. It was not until the renovation of the auditorium that any discernible aesthetic improvement was seen, and that simply called attention to the appearance of the rest of the building.

The charm of West at this time was exterior, the interior was decidedly unattractive.
In the Summer of 1973, it was discovered that the laminated beams in Biester Gym were separating, causing the outside walls to bow out. The beams had to be filled with epoxy and steel reinforcement rods added, a task that took nine months and $200,000 to complete. Physical Education Classes were cancelled, and athletic contests were held at the other Glenbards. A Life-Safety bond issue in 1973 made it possible to replace the cinder and water track with a new and untried surface by 3-M, and to improve the football field after raising the entire field area by four feet.

The work was not completed in time, however, and the football team had to play its games at Glenbard South. The

Homecoming bonfire, which had been revived in 1972, was held in the unpaved school parking lot. The "new" track was used for one season when long strips of the surfacing began peeling away, and the track was "closed" for three years pending the results of litigation against 3-M The school also faced the possibility of having three close neighbors on the hill immediately east of the library when the owner of the land announced plans to develop his property. The Board of Education purchased the land to prevent such a move and soon after, the botanical garden was born. The garden became reality in 1987, though the more developed plans remained in blueprint form only. That area eventually became used for the 2016 science wing. Some citizens tried to thwart the building of the wing due to the trees that would be destroyed with the construction. This effort, however, came at the 11th hour. In the end, construction began--and was completed--on time. Classes met in the new science wing in August 2016.

Glenbard West had begun a program to decorate and brighten the building, but with budget constraints there was little money for anything other than paint. With the assistance of the Art Department, and the classes in Interior Design, wall graphics were painted in the cafeteria, foreign language and mathematics corridors, the girls' gym, and Biester gym.

Pictured left: Brian Diedrich (53) was named Varsity Captain. In 1971, he was the captain of the all-state team. In the picture, he tries to block a punt during the Hilltoppers' 18-0 win over the York Dukes. His jersey is currently on display in GWHS room 416.

Art on the Hilltop

Randy Klackle, (class of 1973), completed the wood relief mural that once was displayed above the main office (picture not found—yet). Beth Humphreys, (class of 1976), added her terra cotta clay bas relief mural in the auditorium lobby (below)

Beth Humphreys wrote, "I loved going to Glenbard West. Mr. Dugoplowski and Mr. DeVeau were AMAZING teachers. I put my heart and soul into that mural. I paid tribute to Mark Stang who had passed, as Hamlet, I am in there as the artist and a good friend of mine, Chris Gies was the juggler. It was HEAVY!"

It was thought to be ceramic, but it is terra cotta clay. The project took her 250 hours to complete.
Pictured below, Beth Humpreys' terra cotta installation in the 1987 Pinnacle. Below left, Beth creates her bas relief—taken from the 1976 Pinnacle.

Clark Tate, (Class of 1977), painted the theater mural on the fourth floor, shown above

.

Bricks from the original building were sold as school memorabilia for $3 each and the resulting profit, along with donations from many school clubs, made possible the planting of 40 trees. The Firley Room, 428, was converted into the Alumni Room, and soon after the Alumni Association was formed for the purpose of "preserving the history and heritage of Glenbard High School." The Association compiled a list of 1,000 alumni names and addresses and collected much of the memorabilia now in the room. The association existed for only three years, but in that time, they did much to kindle interest in the class reunions which have become a popular annual event.

Progress toward enriching the appearance of the building was slowed somewhat in the Fall of 1975 when two boys, both one-time Glenbard West students, broke into the building and caused over $25,000 damage to the library, science rooms, cafeteria, and kitchen. A benevolent court system did not cause either boy to make any restitution or to spend any time in jail, but Glenbard West's insurance rates went up. An opportunity to add to the physical plant and to extend the program was lost when the voters of Glen Ellyn defeated a 1975 Park District bond issue of $1.1 million to build a swimming pool adjoining Biester Gym. In an unusual move, the major taxing bodies Of Glen Ellyn had cooperated to provide a badly needed

Community and school facility. The Village Board was to donate $400,000 they had received from the Federal government for recreational use, the District was to provide the land for the building, provide parking, and pay 55% of the operating costs, and the Park District would propose the bond issue and operate the pool. Additional cost to the average home owner in Glen Ellyn would have been about $6.25 a year. The pool would have been used less than half of the time by the schools and the remainder of the time by the public. A vigorous campaign which featured over 100 coffee presentations in all parts of Glen Ellen was not successful in selling the proposal. It was defeated in every precinct.

The Bicentennial Year was a brighter one for the "Castle." The state approved a proposal to enlarge the library, the first major renovation since 1971; a completely new heating system; and bleachers for the football field. However, a badly needed proposal to increase the building fund was defeated. Also, during the 1976 school year, there was a brief debate on whether graduating seniors should wear red, white, and blue graduation gowns to celebrate America's Bicentennial. In the end, this idea was abandoned and graduation went on with the traditional graduation gown colors: Glenbard green and white. Students asked if the graduation could be held outside on the football field, but the request was denied, and the graduation was held in Biester Gymnasium.

It is not known when the first graduation to be held on Duchon Football Field occurred. With its gorgeous view of Lake Ellyn, every effort has been made to hold graduation outdoors. Pictured, left, a view of graduation from my seat in the faculty section, May 2018.

Two years later, Glenbard West had a new library, complete with a classroom, larger A-V area, isolated stacks, seating for 200 students, and a stained-glass window over the entrance. In June 1987, the library was named the "Robert D. Elliott Library" in honor of the retiring principal.

The bleachers and press box were completed and a year later the Board of Education, with significant financial help from the Boosters Club, added a concession stand, toilets, and team room.

Of course, it is speculation, but it is not probable that Fred L. Biester would have approved permanent football stands. While he was principal, he had the football stands removed at the end of each football season so that there would be an unobstructed view of Lake Ellyn.

At right, Dr. Elliott poses with his portrait. The painting now hangs in the Elliott Library.

The old multicolored radiators which had operated on four different systems were removed and, at a cost of $900,000, students, staff, and faculty could enjoy some uniformity in heat. Lockers were repainted, the suit with 3-M settled, and a new track was installed in 1977.

The replacement of the leaded windows, which were part of the original building, and which had been made in England, caused a minor flap in the community. People were afraid the school would lose its unique appearance as the windows were a part of its charm and character. They were attractive but also drafty and inefficient. All fears were stilled when Thermopane windows which simulated leaded panes were installed. Many of the original windows were sold to interested patrons (probably the same ones who purchased bricks) and the money was put into more trees.

For many years the District offices, housing the superintendent, business manager, and record keeping had been located in the west end of the first floor. (See picture of first floor, left, as it appeared in 2017) This area also served as the meeting room for the Board of Education. It has been evident for some time that this space was totally inadequate for a growing and increasingly sophisticated school district and the move to the present offices on Roosevelt Road was made in the Summer of 1977.

Their removal gave West an opportunity to gain some much-needed space. Work on renovation of the area began in 1977 and continued over the next year. The completed project included rooms for a rapidly expanding program in Special Education, driver education classroom and a simulator laboratory.

Another Life-Safety proposal for 4.4 million dollars to bring all of the Glenbard High Schools into compliance with the newest state safety requirements was approved in January 1984. Fire partitions were erected at each stairwell, smoke and fire alarms were added, fire-resistant carpeting installed, and an elevator was added over a three-year period. A plan to move Radio WGHS to the Park District building in the old Main Street School was found to be too expensive, however, and they had to remain in the tower at Glenbard West after extensive improvements were made.

After so many years and so much effort and money, the building had become quite attractive. Its malevolence was to manifest itself one more time, however, perhaps as a farewell gesture to the retiring principal.

On September 5, 1988, the ceiling in room 326 suddenly let loose and several tons of plaster and debris dropped. There was a class in the room, but the quick action of teacher Ms. Claudia Finley had cleared them out seconds before the collapse. The rails holding the ceiling to the wooden beams had simply let loose; and, while no other ceilings came down, the other 27 rooms in the original wing had the same sort of construction. Amid rumors and considerable media coverage, school was closed for several days while the ceilings were re-anchored.

Claudia Finley 1977

Over the years the students have shown their feelings toward the building in many ways. At a time when it was fashionable to write graffiti on walls and to vandalize schools, Glenbard West's building generally escaped that trend. The school has experienced very little defacing of the building or grounds. Further, the students have shown a respect for the art works in the building.

Graduating Classes have left class gifts that have enhanced the building and campus. The GLENBARD WEST sign on the front hill, (shown at left), wrought iron gates to the Circle drive, Senior Circle, stained glass Windows above the library entrance, in the front stairwell and the fourth-floor lobby, trees in front of Biester gym, clocks and pictures, floor mural in the auditorium lobby, and benches and lighting by the Victory Bell have all come from classes who wanted to leave a lasting gift to their school.

At right, the sign in 1983. At right, a picture of the Glenbard West sign taken with 2007 graduates.

The "Before and After" pictures. An extensive restoration for the Victory Bell began in 2017 and it was rededicated during a ceremony at the September 22, 2018 Homecoming Weekend.

At right, the 1971 yearbook picture, was a gift from the1960 and 1966 graduating classes. The picture on the right features Principal Sheahan in 1971—his last year as principal. The plaque under the bell reads as follows:

THE GLENBARD WEST VICTORY BELL
ORIGINALLY A GIFT FROM THE
CLASSES OF 1960 AND 1966

THE 2018 RESTORATION PROJECT

MAJOR FUNDING FOR THE
BELL RESTORATION PROVIDED BY
THE CLASSES OF 1966, 1967 AND 1968

NEW SUPPORT FRAME DONATED BY
THE CLASS OF 1984

RESTORATION AND ENHANCEMENT
OF THE PEDESTAL
A GIFT FROM THE CLASS OF 2018

An essential part of the continuing success and quest for excellence at Glenbard West has been the constant and active support of its parents and the Glenbard community. They have voted for higher taxes to maintain a high quality of education, and they have donated their time and talents in many other ways. This book would not be complete without highlighting and acknowledging the support of the parents and community members.

The Boosters Club has continued to grow and to increase both its moral and financial support to all school organizations who seek its help. The Band Parents have been a major factor in the rejuvenation of the band program and were instrumental in the successful band trips to the Peach Bowl in 1984, and to Los Angeles in 1986. The Citizens Advisory Council, while always small in numbers, has served as an invaluable sounding board for new ideas and policies and has been a supportive critic in those areas where performance was below expectations. Most important, these groups have allowed the school officials to "run their own show" and have not sought to dictate policy or rule on personnel matters.

President Bill and Joy Tuburk

Past President Brian and Deb Diver

First Vice President Rich and Mary Yangas

Second Vice President Mike and Linda Sear

Treasurer Dave and Maureen Petersen

Secretary Fran Morof

Principal, Glenbard West High School Dr. Peter Monaghan

Superintendent, District 87 Dr. David Larson

2016-2017: Room 400 becomes the new Writing Center

At right, the 1984 wall murals in room 400 were painted by Chris Wahlgren. The room was used as a classroom until the fall of 2016. It was converted into a writing center.

As the 2016-17 English Department attempted to turn room 400 into a writing center, one English teacher, Mrs. Carolyn Fritts, asked her student, Louie Wahlgren, if he had an Uncle Chris. He said that he did not, but that he did have an Aunt Chris. After confirming that she was the very same Chris Wahlgren that painted the mural, we were able to contact her via email. What follows (on the next page) is an email written by Chris Wahlgren. It is reprinted here, with her permission.

May 31, 2017

For the gifted program in 1983-84 with Miss Carroll, we were each asked to do a big project. I had Miss Dill's British Literature class in Room 400 that year, but the mural in the room at that time was unfinished -- I think it might have been the Canterbury Tales or something else set out in the woods. I decided to do a new mural as my project.

My mom and I painted it over my spring break junior year using acrylic paint. It was an ambitious project for me, especially since I hadn't used acrylic paint much before. I was originally going to make a long row of figures looking over the classroom like in some Renaissance murals I'd researched, but my mom suggested cutting down the number of figures so it wouldn't take as long to paint.

My mom, Kay Wahlgren, is an artist who teaches watercolor at the DuPage Art League, so she helped me plan things out and showed me how to mix the paints. We decided to mimic the Gothic look of the school's exterior in the mural. My mom painted the arches and bricks, and I sketched out and painted the figures. It took about five days to paint the whole thing, and we were pretty sore from standing on ladders and painting over our heads. The hardest part was figuring out how to paint the knight's armor to look like shiny metal.

My nephew Louis said you were looking for information about who the characters are.

Eliza Doolittle from *Pygmalion*

The Time Traveler from *The Time Machine*

The Friar from *The Canterbury Tales*

Sherlock Holmes

William Shakespeare

A knight and his lady

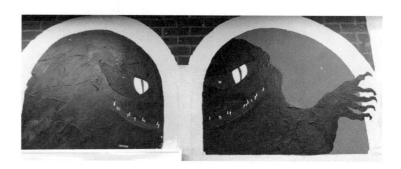

Grendel from Beowulf …attacking the loudspeaker, which kept going off even over Spring break.

I graduated in 1985 and majored in English Lit at Carleton College, graduating in 1989. I got my master's degree in Library and Information Science in 2010 and now work as a reference librarian. Glenbard West prepared me well for college, and I still like walking down by Lake Ellyn and seeing the school on the hill.

Sincerely,

Christine Wahlgren Edison

Glenbard West has an effective, talented, caring faculty who have demonstrated their ability to bring students to the highest academic standards while maintaining a sense of humor, empathy and understanding of students, and the ability to cope with the idiosyncrasies of the building. Teachers and parents have the joy of working with a talented student body, the finest in America. All of the ingredients for success are present and, as Glenbard West approached its 75th birthday, it can look back with pride on its accomplishments, and to its future with confidence and trust.

This ends the narrative of Glenbard West High School, written for the 75th Anniversary.

What follows is a timeline of events that have occurred since then.

1990's: Teachers' Strike, The Great Fire, and The Great Flood

1998: The GEA (teacher's union) and District 87 School Board cannot come to terms with the new teacher contract. The teachers vote to strike, delaying the start of school for one week. The strike is finally settled after a car plows into teachers marching at Glenbard South High School. No one is injured, but a settlement comes quickly after that.

Dr. Pam Zimmermann is named the 8th principal. After her tenure at GWHS, she moves to the Dist. 87 administrative office where she serves as assistant superintendent of instruction.

2006: Dr. Jane Thorsen is named the 9th principal. During her time at Glenbard West, she helped with the following:
- Double-digit increase in the number of students enrolled in AP courses.
- Record high average ACT composite score
- The greatest increase in Prairie State Achievement Exam reading scores in DuPage County
- A volunteer-driven capital campaign to provide a lighted, artificial turf field: Memorial Field
- A record number of students participating in sports and extra-curricular activities

At right, a scary day. On May 9, 2007, towards the end of the school day, an electrical transformer caught fire. The fire destroyed wiring in the building.

The school was closed as crews were sent to repair and clean the building. Classes resumed on Tuesday, May 15, 2007. Photo by Bruce Medic.

April 18, 2013: The District Office closes all Glenbard schools due to flooding. The website read as follows:

SCHOOLS ARE CLOSED:
Due to flooding and road conditions, all Glenbard high schools and the Glenbard District 87 administration center will be closed today April 18, 2013.

2000's: New Science Wing Added and All Students have iPads

Dr. Peter Monaghan, who started at GWHS as a dean, becomes the 10th principal of the school.

GWHS football team has a winning season, but loses to Wheaton-Warrenville South in the State Championships

GWHS football team wins State Championship.

2015-2016 The science wing is added. Construction begins in the fall of 2015.

In the fall of 2016, school opens with a new science wing—and air conditioning in the entire building. It is the first addition since 1964. Also, the school year opens with all students having iPads. Schoology is used for all classes and students use Google Drive.

In May 2017, Girls' Track and Field win Glenbard West's first ever State Championship.

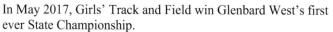

On March 14, 2018, students stage a walk-out at 10am for 17 minutes to commemorate the 17 victims of the Marjory Stoneman Douglas High School shooting. Said GWHS Senior, Grace Bouton, "It bothers me when people say, 'I don't want to walk out because it won't change anything' This is a nationwide movement. I don't want guns in this school, and I don't want the teachers to be armed. I don't want those 17 kids to go down as just another school shooting." It was the first student protest at Glenbard West since 1970.

The following information was researched, gathered, and written by Music Teacher, Mr. Bill Ortega.

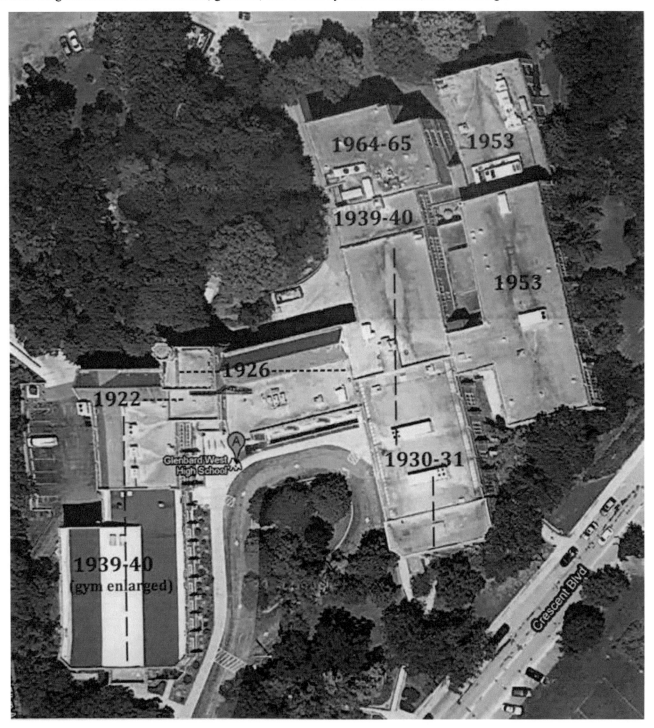

1922: The Original School

> Everything west of the tower, but only 1st through 4th floors. The 5th and 6th floor classrooms were added later. The Hilltop Gym existed but was not yet expanded to its current size.

1927: A new addition to the school opened

- 1963 yearbook clearly states the area west of the current auditorium was added between the tower and current auditorium. This is sometimes referred to as the "Tower Addition."
- It appears the 5th and 6th floors of the tower were added later. Careful study of the exterior brickwork clearly shows the original building and where the 1926 addition occurs.
- A single pre-1926 photo exists in room 400—the Alumni Room—showing the original entrance.

1930-31: The auditorium and wing to the north of the auditorium are built

- Stone on side of Auditorium reads "1930." The 1963 yearbook confirms this.
- The original gym (Hilltop Gym) contained a stage which was taken out when the current Auditorium was built. Four unfinished classrooms were completed (1939-1940 addition).
- 4th floor was added later???
- Exterior 4th floor brickwork above cafeteria kitchen clearly does not match floors 2 and 3.

1938: An addition to the high school was approved

- 1963 yearbook mentions an addition to the foods area which is consistent with this area being part of the cafeteria.
- The Hilltop Gym was expanded around this time.

1953: A new addition is built. See the 1953 *Pinnacle* for pictures.

1958: Biester Gymnasium built

1964: Music/Science wing

- Appears in the 1964 and 1965 *Pinnacle* yearbooks.
- 4th floor added to 1939-40 addition??
- These two 4th floor classrooms were added, but it is unclear when.

1965: New lunch facilities. See the 1965 *Pinnacle*.

1971: Auditorium remodeled. Details of the remodel:

- Wooden-backed seats replaced with plastic-backed seats
- Stage extended into the audience, side panels added that block out a set of windows
- 1971 Pinnacle yearbook mentions the "soon to occur" remodel job as well as showing a picture. The 1972 Pinnacle mentions the remodel job after the fact. The following remnants of the old auditorium can still be seen:
  - Original tile under the stage
  - Original windows behind side, diagonal wall extensions
  - Original proscenium visible from cove and through wall extensions.

1972: Biester Gymnasium remodeled due to structural failure in the roof

2001: Field House added to Biester Gymnasium

2016: Science Wing: The East side of the school was hillside, left wild and named The Zahrobsky Garden. Because it would have cost millions to build, the plans were drawn up, but it was never started. In the fall of 2015, the work began on the addition, cutting down trees and removing tons of dirt from the hillside.

The Ten Principals: Glen Ellyn High School, Glenbard High School, Glenbard West High School

#1: Arthur Holtzman served from 1915-1918. Glen Ellyn High School's first principal. Holzman served when classes were still meeting in the DuPage County Bank at the corner of Main and Crescent. He resigned in May 1918 to enter military service after quite a bit of controversy. (See page 8 for a more detailed explanation.) The United States declared war on the German Empire on April 6, 1917. World War I officially ended on November 11, 1918 at 11:00am. We currently celebrate Veteran's Day on November 11.

#2: Fred L. Biester served as principal from 1918 to 1957. In July 1957, he was named Superintendent of Glenbard High School District 87. It was Biester who brought the students over from the bank building to the new school in April 1923. After holding a contest to name the school, the name GLENBARD was chosen from a student entry. Biester is considered the Father of Glenbard High School. The school was officially dedicated on May 15, 1923.

#3: David H. Miller served as principal from 1957-1961. When school started in the fall of 1957, Glenbard High School became Glenbard WEST High School. Glenbard East opened to 9th and 10th grade only.

#4: John D. Sheahan served as principal from 1961-1971. Prior to becoming the 4th principal, Mr. Sheahan served as principal of a high school for US Air Force dependents in Wiesbaden, Germany. He then became assistant principal at Willowbrook High School, according to the 1962 *Pinnacle.*

#5: William Dutch served as interim principal from 1972- January 1972. He was an assistant principal at GWHS before serving as assistant superintendent.

#6: Dr. Robert Elliott served as principal from January 1972-1987. During his tenure as principal, Twentieth Century Fox filmed *Lucas* at the school. It premiered in March 1986. Dr. Elliott also eliminated the Valedictorian/Salutatorian tradition, creating the new Senior Honors Medal. Before coming to GWHS, Dr. Elliott was assistant superintendent at Oak Park-River Forest High School.

#7: Dr. Susan J. Bridge served as principal from 1987-1999. Dr. Bridge earned her doctorate degree for her work on the history of Glenbard District 87. During her tenure as principal, MTV shot the TV series, *Yearbook,* at the high school, homes, and areas around Glenbard West. *Yearbook* was one of the earliest experiments in "reality TV." Following her time at GWHS, she became the superintendent of Oak Park-River Forest High School.

#8: Dr. Pamela Zimmerman served as principal from 1999-2006. Coming from Stevenson High School, Dr. Zimmerman's tenure, the PLC (Professional Learning Community) came into existence well as an increase of students taking more Advanced Placement classes and tests

#9: Dr. Jane Thorsen served as principal from 2006-2013. During her time as principal, GWHS ranked the 5th best high school in Illinois on a list compiled by *The Washington Post* in 2012. Dr. Thorsen had a 34-year career in education when she retired in 2013.

#10: Dr. Peter Monaghan is currently serving as principal, having begun in 2013. He earned his doctorate degree while serving as principal. He has started as a dean of students. He then became the Assistant Principal of Student Services. During his tenure, the addition of the science wing became a reality—the first time since the 1960's that academic classrooms were added to the high school.

Hilltopper Sports

Since the first Pinnacle yearbook did not arrive until 1940, we need to start with that year as we tell the story of the high school's athletic teams. During the 1940's teams are called by various names, such as:

- The Green Wave
- The Bardites
- The Green and White
- The Bards
- The Glenbard Boys
- The Toppers
- The Hilltoppers. This nickname can be found in the 1940 Pinnacle, but it is uncertain when it was coined or by whom.

Pictured, below, the 1940 Tennis team.

Coach Ralph Magor, left, coached the boys' team.

The girls' team, coached by Cornelia Barth, (shown at right) provided the only interscholastic sport open to girls. Members were chosen through elimination tournaments. In 1972, Title IX opened the door to interscholastic sports for girls.

State Championships

It should be noted that Glenbard West has had many, many individual State Champions. But one man, Fred Beilfuss, needs to be mentioned here. In 1966, he was the first State Champion in the history of the school. No other team or individual had won a State Championship before Fred did it in wrestling. To honor his achievement, the school held a special Convo—but he was not informed in advance. In a 2019 interview, Fred said that he had planned to skip school that day, but he decided to go anyway. Good thing he went to school: the entire student body gathered in the auditorium to celebrate his success, the band played, and Fred gave a speech.

Glenbard West High School Team State Championships

1960 Boys Cross Country

1983 Girls Volleyball

1983 Football

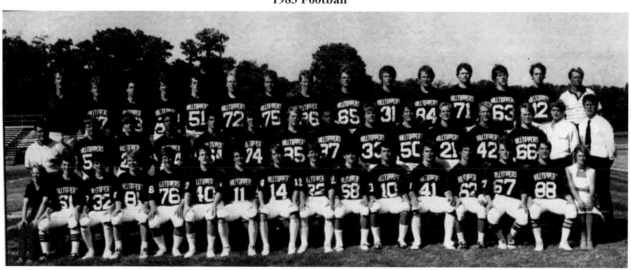

1996 Boys Gymnastics

2012 Football

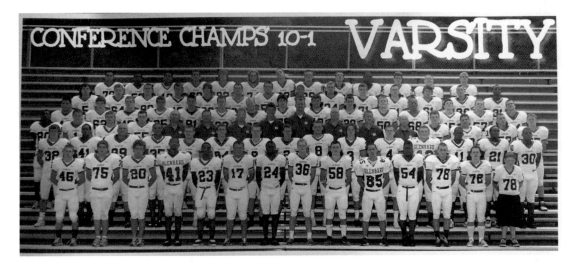

2013 Girls' Cross Country

2015 Football

2015 Boys Volleyball

2016 Boys Volleyball

2016 Girls Track and Field Combined

2017 Boys Gymnastics

2017 Girls Track and Field

2017 Boys Volleyball

2018 Girls Gymnastics

1940

Football: Divided into Heavyweights and Lightweights.

Basketball: Divided into Heavyweights and Lightweights.

Track: This sport was available for boys only.

Boys' Intramurals and Girls' Intramurals: This was competitive, but only within the high school.

Tennis: This sport was unique in that it was available for interscholastic competition for both girls and boys.

Golf: A boys only sport.

Girls' Gym. From the 1940 Pinnacle, "Although girls cannot participate in interscholastic sports, with the exception of tennis, they find a wide varied field open to them in gym classes. In the fall here is hockey for upperclassmen and soccer for freshmen. This is followed by basketball, which is carried on through the winter. Between basketball and volley ball a program of varied sports, mainly badminton and table tennis, is carried out. Volley ball and baseball constitute the spring program. In this connection, class tournaments are held as is a soccer contest in the fall. Several girls go out for tennis. To further an interest in sports the G.A.A (Girls' Athletic Association) holds classes in archery and horseback riding.

Cheerleading: Not recognized as a sport or club, but cheerleaders are mentioned in the 1940 Pinnacle. While girls mostly comprised the cheerleading squads, there are instances of boys joining cheerleading, such as in the 1949 Pinnacle. See picture, right.

1945
Cross Country begins at Glenbard. The team placed 5th in the conference. It is boys only.

Football note: In 1945, Football and Basketball no longer divides between Heavyweights and Lightweights. Varsity and Frosh-Soph are the new names.

1947
Baseball begins. Glenbard's first game was played on April 11, 1947. Pictured, is the 1948 team. The 1947 Pinnacle did not include a picture of the 1947 team.

1958
Intramural Wrestling begins for boys. Also, a Boys' Bowling League begins.

1959
Varsity Wrestling and Frosh-Soph Wrestling has their first seasons. Pictured, below.

Gymnastics: Open to boys only. Begins as an intramural sport in 1959. In 1960, a full year of meets are scheduled.

1969

Swimming. From the 1969 Pinnacle, "Glenbard West High School unfortunately has no swimming pool but we do have a swimming team—technically. And the team, consisting of senior Roy Schlachter, a 50-yard free stylist, placed 19th in the State preliminaries, pictured at right. Our Glenbard tankster team was organized when Roy found the YMCA competition too lean and entered the State swim meet under Glenbard West. His school sponsor is Mrs. Delores Langston, physical education instructor.

Important Date in Glenbard Sports: June 23, 1972: Title IX is a comprehensive federal law that prohibits discrimination on the basis of sex in any federally funded education program or activity.

1972

Girls' Gymnastics: Six West Suburban Conference teams competed in this initial year of girls' gymnastics, and Glenbard's girls ranked fourth in the conference. Pictured, Wendy Toyama from the 1977 Pinnacle. Wendy was the first female Glenbardian to make it to the State Meet.

1973

Girls' Track: Four girls qualified for the State Finals as Glenbard's first Girls Interscholastic Track Team scored 40 points and took second place in the District Track Meet held at Conant High School.

1974

Archery: The girls' team competed and won the West Suburban Conference meet held at Riverside Brookfield High School—despite being winless in the regular season.

Girls' Swim Team: Swimmers Chris Hoffman, Nancy Hooper, and Debbie Patterson put Glenbard West on the national sports map when they helped the B.R. Ryall YMCA capture the 1974 YMCA National Championship in Fort Lauderdale, Florida in April.

1976

Girls' Basketball: In their first year of competition in the West Suburban Conference, the Girls' Basketball team outscored six straight opponents and captured the Conference Crown. They enjoyed an undefeated (8-0) season. Pictured, the 1976 Girls' Basketball team.

Girls' Volleyball: Although the Girls' Volleyball team started their first season of interscholastic competition with a victory over Glenbard South, the girls never won another game, finishing 1-8 for the season.

`1977

Girls' Softball: In their first season of interscholastic competition, the Girls' Softball Team (5-7) finished fourth in the West Suburban Conference and placed two players on the All-Conference team.

1979

Girls' Cross Country: The Girls' Cross Country Team took first place at the Crystal Lake Invitational, considered by some coaches to be the unofficial State Cross Country Meet. The week before, the team came in second at the Downers Grove North Invitational, which was also billed as the unofficial state meet. The conflicting claims for the title of unofficial state meet were never really resolved. The Crystal Lake Invitational was sanctioned by the United States Track and Field Federation and was called the USTFF Girls' Cross Country Championship. The Downers Grove North Invitational was endorsed by Track and Field News and Timely Times. The approval of an official state cross country meet for girls was in the hands of the IHSA—the Illinois High School Association.

1980

Boys' Soccer: The very first soccer team in the history of the school did it better than most of their competitors in the West Suburban Conference. Competing at the junior varsity level, the Hilltoppers took second place in the final standings. Their overall record was 5-7-2.

1981

Boys' Soccer: This was the first season of interscholastic varsity competition. The Hilltoppers were 2-18-1. They finished 8th in the West Suburban Conference.

1988

Girls Soccer: After much discussion between parents, administration, and the School Board, West was supported by a new girls' soccer team. And the team excelled in its first season. Team members worked hard through many muddy practices in early spring, and their dedication and aggressiveness paid off during the season. The team ended the season with a conference record of 5-3 and an overall record of 11-5-3.

1994

Topperettes began as a club in 1965. In the 1993-1994 school year, the group is known as Dance Squad. Pictured, below left, the 1966 Topperettes. Below right, is most likely Alison Garelick. (The photo came from the 1994 *Pinnacle*, but no name was given.)

1999
Badminton: This girls' sport began a fabulous first season. The team sent several players to conference. 25 girls played on this inaugural year—including Liz Meyer and Kari Deger who almost went to state.

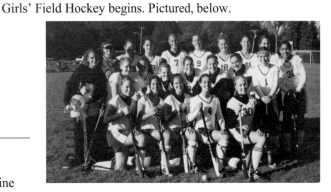

2002
Ice Hockey: Listed as a sport in 2002, Ice Hockey is featured as a boys' sport

2004
Rugby, (boys' sport) begins.

Boys' Lacrosse begins. Pictured, below.

2005
Girls' Field Hockey begins. Pictured, below.

2006
Boys' Volleyball: The varsity team's first year is led by nine seniors, junior, and a sophomore.

2010
Girls' Lacrosse begins its inaugural season. Pictured, right.

Clubs and Student Organizations

The descriptions come directly from various *Pinnacle* editions.

1940
Girl Reserves: Often referred to as G.R. Open to any girl who wishes to join. A high school YWCA Club with service as its general purpose.

Girls' Athletic Association: The GAA was the largest club in the school. The program was not limited to sports. There was also interest in sports, good health, and good sportsmanship.

Hi-Y: Similar to the Girl Reserves, Hi-Y is the high school branch of the YMCA. Any boy who agrees to live up to the platform of clean living, clean athletics, clean speech, and clean scholarship may join.

Art Club: Organized to promote interest in art. As a side line, the club earns money with candy, popcorn-ball, and taffy apple sales to improve the art room. In 1940, the Art Club raised nearly $75. Funds were used to buy scissors, new vases, artificial flowers, and tools for carving wood and linoleum blocks.

Kits and Skits: The goal was to promote an interest in drama and the theater. They believed that this goal could not be achieved by the Thespians, as the new members each year are chosen in connection with the class plays, and they club couldn't be started before spring.

Thespians: An honorary society for high school dramatists. It is officially known as Troupe Number 233 of the National Thespians.

French Club: Promoted more interest in the French people and the events taking place in France, and to furnish opportunities for use of the language outside of class

Spanish Club: Since the local branches of the student Pan American League are organized to promote interest in the countries of Latin America and friendliness between North and South America, the Spanish club is part of a wide-spread organization. During the year, several discussions are held on the subject of Pan American unity and how to promote it.

Latin Club: When an aspiring Latin student takes it upon himself to enroll in the third year of the language, he finds himself automatically a member of the Latin Club. One day early in October, he comes to school attired in Roman garb; and after escorted through the Underworld, he becomes a full-fledged member of the club.

Science Club: Way off in the corner of the building, far enough from the office, the auditorium, and the cooking class to be safe, meets the small but patient science club. Some of the outstanding meeting this year were a talk on radio, with a discussion of frequency, modulation and various police radio systems, and talks on welding, machinery and growing plants with chemicals.

Library Staff: Behind the scenes, or rather behind the desk in the library, is a group of juniors and seniors who aid the librarian in carding and shelving books.

Glen Bard **Staff:** This group of students were responsible for publishing the school newspaper. The staff was chosen from a large group who wrote several stories in the tryouts. The first printed high school paper was Glen-Hi. It was published in February 1919.

Pinnacle **Staff:** Responsible for the planning, copy writing, and setting up of plates for the school yearbook.

"G" Club: An honorary society of Glenbard athletes, holds the distinction of being the most exclusive club in school. In order to become a member, a boy must have been awarded one heavyweight or lightweight letters, have the unanimous approval of the faculty advisers, and receive a vote of at least seventy-five per cent of the club. The purpose is to encourage high team morale, high ideals, clean athletics and good sportsmanship.

Athletic Association: Its major purpose is to stimulate student interest in sports and promote the financial success of athletic events. It is empowered to call pep meeting any time the president feels the student interest to be lagging.

1941

Aeronauts: A group of model airplane builders. At the bi-weekly meetings the members discuss their own problems and matier in "Air Trails" magazine.

Ipso Facto: One of the most exclusive clubs at Glenbard, it is composed of the presidents (sixteen in all) of every school -sponsored club at Glenbard. Money is furnished by numerous candy and hot dog sales throughout the school year. (Many is the time when those wieners and buns tasted good.) Pictured, right.

Town Meeting Group: A forum based upon the Town Meeting radio program. The only requirement for membership is a vital interest in current affairs and the desire to actively discuss them. Meetings were held at 8pm on Thursdays.

Masque and Gavel: A national honorary speech organization for the recognition and encouragement of those showing superior ability in oral speech in the classroom, convocation, or city.

Junior Izaac Waltons: A club affiliated with and supported by the DuPage Chapter of Senior Izaac Walton League of America. Their purpose is conservation of American woods, waters, and wildlife. They are later referred to as "Junior Ikes."

1942

Student Cabinet: Consisted of the presidents of the Hi-Y, G.R., G.A.A. and Athletic Association as well as those of the four classes. Helped with school affairs as well as aiding the defense program by selling defense stamps during the noon hour.

Chess Club: This club was open to any member desiring to play chess. It began in 1941, but it did not appear in Pinnacle until 1942.

1943: No new clubs.

1944

Quill and Scroll: Open to juniors and seniors, the Quill and Scroll is the international honorary society for high school journalists. Membership is a sign of outstanding journalistic endeavor.

Radio Club: Entrusted with the care and operation of the school's sound equipment, the club conducts a class in radio theory to provide capable operators and maintenance men.

1945: No new clubs.

1946

Electronics Club: Radio and electronics are the main interests of these boys who meet once a month for study and practical experience. The project for 1946 was a five-tube shortwave set build by the boys themselves. (Note: this club had to wait until the end of WWII when the air waves were once again opened to amateurs.)

1947

Student Council: This group gathered in Room 316 second period every day. They are commonly known as the Student Council. Besides taking care of small but very important jobs in and out of the building, that year's council gave the school a flag, a bulletin board for extra-curricular activities, and a suggestion box.

Y-Teens: The purpose is to promote a spirit of fellowship and service among the girls at Glenbard. To further these ideals the big and little sister plan was continued, and on Thanksgiving, toys and games were sent to needy children.

Camera Club: The club had meetings once a month for which the program committee secured speakers who presented various fundamental on photographing and developing.

Archery Club: The group meet once a month to discuss the various phases of archery, hunting, roving and target shooting. The club hoped to use the shop in the winter to make and repair its own archery equipment.

1948 and 1949: No new clubs.

1950

Red Cross Council: Although Glenbard has had no explosions, floods, train wrecks, fires, or epidemics, the Junior Red Cross carried out many projects. They initiated a welcoming committee for bewildered Bards enrolling during the school year, made Thanksgiving window transparencies for children's wards, made nut cups and cribbage boards for veterans, and to top it off, send over 1,000 Christmas cards from the student body to veterans' hospitals.

History Club: The club was formed so that history students, who desired to, might learn more about all phases of this field.

Pep Club: The purpose of Pep Club was to promote better sportsmanship and to encourage better school spirit among the students. To be eligible for membership one must be a girl—and be enthusiastic. The members of the club made green and white pompoms and wore green and white mittens to urge their teams on to victory.

Science Club: This club studied and discussed all field of modern science. Science Clubbers learned about chemistry, glass blowing, liquid air, geology and hidden radio transmitter hunts. The February meeting was spent watching the biology students dissect frogs.

1951

Pan American League: Formerly known as the Spanish Club. It is known as P.A.L.

1952

Girls' Pep Club: Known as "Lusty Lunged Ladies." Cheering the teams on to victory and togged in green and white, members of the three-year old Girls' Pep Club were eligible for awards if they attended three-fourths of the conference games. Attendance was taken by the class heads. (This club first appeared in the 1952 Pinnacle.

Boys' Pep Club: Known as "Lusty Lunged Lads." This group promoted better spirit and sportsmanship at Glenbard. The club's biggest project was to collect the wood for the Homecoming bonfire.

Sound, Projection, Stage Crew Club: Known as S.P.S.C. This was an organization made up of skilled technicians who worked behind the scenes in Glenbard's convos. In 1952, they acquired a new tape-recording machine.

Dance Club: Students met to learn social dancing and square dancing. The group met at Forest Glen School.

1953

Monitors: Glenbard's Monitors, organized in the spring of 1952, were instituted to help maintain order in the school's halls. Their duties included removing unlocked locks and emptying unlocked lockers, directing visitors around the school, and checking student passes.

monitors

student office help

Student Office Help. This club first year it appeared in Pinnacle in 1953, but it was the 1957 Pinnacle that described the club as a service organization consisting of 23 girls who aided regular office staff. Group members collect, sort, and deliver attendance cards, extra slips, pink passes, and notes we well as running errands for teachers. They are in charge of the ticket booth during the lunch periods. These girls learned about the operation of business offices.

1954

Current Events Club: Formed in 1954 for all of Glenbard's future politicians. It was the first opportunity that Glenbardians have ever had for debate and was open to anyone who wished to discuss the current problems of the day.

1955

790 Club: Besides aiding Glenbard's bookworms, we had the duties of stamping and mending books, straightening shelves, and keeping the library in good working order. (Perhaps this was the new name of the Library Club.) As the 1958 Pinnacle describes, the name of the club comes from the types of books in the Dewey Decimal System's 790's section—games and pure fun.

Electronics Club: At the meetings, the Electronics Club demonstrated various types of electronic equipment and explained their uses. The club's purpose was to share knowledge with each other and relieve S.P.S.C. of some of their many responsibilities.

Future Teachers of America: Also known as F.T.A. This club provided interested students with information about teaching and the colleges which could best prepare them for a teaching career. Since each branch of the national organization is named for an outstanding member of its respective community, FTA decided to name its branch the Fred L. Biester Future Teachers of America.

1956

Smoking Council: Elimination of smoking from Glenbard's campus is the purpose of Smoking Council. Advised by Mr. Miller (the principal at the time), the Council issued and enforced smoking regulations and punished violators.

Inter-Club Council: This club was formed to co-ordinate the activities of Glenbard's largest girls' clubs.

Youth Center: This club promoted and sponsored intra-and inter-school socials and mixers, held dances, and provided a place and activities for student "get togethers."

L'Alliance Francaise: The new name of French Club.

Projection Crew: They operated all movie projection equipment.

Mathematics Club: Discussion and solving of problems in different phases of mathematics, including calculus, which are not covered in the classroom was the purpose of Math Club. Interest in math was stimulated and members were encouraged to enter math contests.

Ferroequinologitsts: This is the fancy name for Railroad Club. Meetings featured trips to railroad installations, railroad yards, and other railroad clubs as well as movies and speakers.

Astronomy: Star-gazing and building a new telescope were the activities of Astronomy Club.

Square Dance Club: Promotion and participation in square dancing. It also included folk dancing.

Civil Air Patrol: Also known as C.A.P., this club was an auxiliary of the United States Air Force set up to teach the social, political, economic, international, and vocational facets of aviation. Activities included flying a Pinnacle photographer over the school to take an aerial picture.

1957
Magic Club: Organized on November 6, 1956, the "Prestidigitators" were organized to give Glenbard students, who have a sincere interest in magic, an opportunity to learn more about magic. Their meetings were planned to give every member a chance to show and improve his repertoire of deceptive tricks.

Glenbard Technical Service Crew: Took care of staging, lights, projection, and sound. It is also known as G.T.S.C.

1958
Helladians: This was an honor society for student who had made outstanding contributions to Glenbard in the fields of architecture, design, display, and fine arts.

Hi-C: The purpose of Hi-C is to present to teenagers the real Christian way of life.

Young Life: The purposes were to enjoy living as much as possible and to find out what makes life click. This was done by bringing the principles of Christianity to bear on the lives of the high school people. There requirements for coming to Young Life Club were two-fold. Members were required to be young—and alive.

1959
Boating Club: The Boat Club strove to fulfill their purpose—to promote interest and enjoyment in boating knowledge of safety, and to develop navigational skills for better and safer boating, throughout the school year. Members were required to know how to swim. They also had to own a boat or become a partner in ownership with a present member.

Student Court: This was an off-shoot of Campus Council. Student Court composed of the officers and monitor heads. There were able to judge violations and give penalties for offences.

Debate Club: Launched officially at 3:29pm on November 11, 1958, Debate Club began.

Glenbard Senior Girl Scouts: In September 1958, the Senior Girl Scouts at Glenbard joined together to form a club known as Glenbard Senior Girl Scouts. It was formed as a service organization to aid Glenbard in any way possible.

G-Club: This club is composed of all boys who earned the official varsity letter. The object of the club was to provide an honorary organization for Glenbard athletes and to encourage a high type of team morale. Some duties of the G-Club are to keep order at the pep convos, to hold ropes and maintain order at home basketball games, and to sponsor the G-Club Faculty basketball game.

Nurse's Aids: No information is given, but they do appear in the 1959 Pinnacle.

1960: No new clubs.

1961
Phi Beta Chi: The new name of the Science Club

1962
Der Deutsche Verein: Also known as German Club: This club provided opportunities for interested German students to extend their knowledge of Germany—its people and customs—by forming study groups in music, literature, and the arts, and by celebrating three German holidays.

Pep Rally Committee: An off-shoot of the Pep Club

Round Table: Formerly known as the Current Events Club

Yacht Club: Formerly known as the Boat Club

1963: No new clubs

1964

Knights of the Plume: Glenbard West's writing society. Stimulates literary creativity through informal group appraisal of the writings of its members. The literary magazine was The Id. Of special note: one of the officers was Larry Shue. He later went on to write the plays The Nerd and The Foreigner. (Read more about Larry Shue in the Notable Alumni section of this book.)

1965

Ski Club: Enjoying the heavy snows of the winter, the members of Ski Club took advantage of the white slopes to improve upon their skiing. Such techniques as the schuss, skiing straight downhill without slowing or turning, and the Christie, a method of turning and stopping were evidenced in the more experienced skiers.

Mu Alpha Theta: A national honorary mathematics society. Members explore the areas of mathematics that are not ordinarily covered in the classrooms.

G-Teens: A girls' club devoted to serving peoples of the world. Members fulfilled this purpose by taking in various service projects such as: the filling of Christmas stockings, visiting convalescent homes, and supplying food for needy families. G-Teens also sponsored the Candlelight Service, the Big and Little Sister Tea, The Mother-Daughter Banquet, and annual boy-ask-girl formal, the Heart Hop.

Cinema Club: If you are looking for an entertaining afternoon, the Cinema Club is the right place. Cinema Club has the most outstanding movies in movie history. Covering almost all of the different aspects of movies, Cinema Club never complains of boredom.

Rifle Club: No description was given until 1967. The 1967 Pinnacle description reads as follows: "Rifle Club tries to instill its members with proper respect and usage of weapons for recreational use."

RIFLE CLUB

IIR: The brainstorm of senior Jean Williams and advisor Con C. Patsavas, is the only club in Glenbard without a single member. The people in the picture have merely participated in one or more of the IIR sponsored events. While IIR has no set membership, there are always some eager Toppers who have an interest in various lecture seminars on underdeveloped nations or current world affairs. (It was not clear from descriptions in Pinnacle what "IIR" stood for or meant.)

Castle Players: Throughout the year (1964-65), Castle Players, sponsored a dance, built a Homecoming float, presented a convo play, sponsored a trip to see the "Madwoman of Chaillot," and conducted an oral interpretations contest.

Literary Society: The new name for Knights of the Plum started in 1964. In 1965, the literary magazine was revived from its moribund condition in some hidden dusty archive known only to the ivy-covered walls. Every Tuesday afternoon, the members of the society met to discuss the merits of the various rhetorical and poetical masterpieces which ordinarily would be filed in the most common of round archives. The publication date was set for May 1965 for the indirect descendent of The Bard of the 1930's.

SENIOR BOYS CHEERING SECTION

Senior Boys Cheering Section: At first glance they may just look like a heterogeneous group of campus wheels, but a second glance will tell the full story, for these young men will be chanting one of their favorite cheers such as the ever popular "Down in Front." One of the groups largely responsible for the upsurge in school spirit here at Glenbard has been the Senior Boys' Cheering Section. Without any recognized leadership, the boys have managed to inspire not only the crowds, but the football and basketball teams with their impromptu chants and animated cheers.

Future Nurses Club: This club was organized to incite interest in the various fields of nursing by informing students of the opportunities, qualifications, and paths to modern nursing.

1966

Key Club: A service club, Key Club was sponsored by Kiwanis, not the school. Activities included washing police cars, helping with Kiwanis's Peanut Day, and a soap drive for Dixon.

Topperettes: This began as a club in 1965—a precursor of the Dance Squad. The 1965 Pinnacle description reads as follows: "This year's new half-time entertainers, The Topperettes, find it necessary to practice twice a week regularly, and as often as possible the week before a performance, to perfect their chorus line uniformity. Having survived the try-outs and making their own uniforms, the Topperettes are continually practicing new and different acts.

Visual Arts Club: Also known as V.A.C. This group merged two other clubs: Camera Club and the Art Club.

Topper's Stompers: The new name of the Square-Dancing Club.

1967

Bridge Club: The popularity of Bridge invaded the high school ranks in 1967. Not only the students, but also many faculty members were among the many Glenbardians who enjoyed Bridge—which is not based solely on luck. In 1968, the Pinnacle reported that Bridge Club had a tournament with Willowbrook.

Chem Club: Students who acquired a liking for chemistry, either in school or on their own, had an opportunity to expand their knowledge of chemistry. These students were easily recognized by their burgundy sweatshirts, which are available only to those students who are eligible to, and have joined, this club of future chemists.

Forerunners Ushering Club: This club was organized in 1965. It began as a small group from the home economics classes. The members usher at all school events, including plays, concerts parents' night, and college night. Of special note, Nancy Derk, president of Forerunners Club, became CEO of Fox Searchlight Pictures. Read more about her in the Notable Alumni section of this book.

'Lectron League: The new name of the Electronics Club

Orchesis: This club is for girls who like dancing. The club consists of two groups: the novices (for beginners) and the concert group, which performs for various clubs and organizations throughout the year. No lessons are necessary, it's all for fun.

1968

All Nighters Club: Meeting on various nights to engage in twelve-hour poker parties, the All-Nighters had many memorable moments. Among some of the occurrences that may be mentioned here are the now infamous Jack of Spades-seven of Diamonds incident, and the Mystery of the Calcium Deposits of the Thirteen Ball. The highlight of every evening was the presentation of the "Howie of the Week" Award, given to the person who best demonstrated the personal qualities of those of John Houk. Needless to say, John won this award nearly always.

Russian Club: This club was organized with the purpose of gaining a deeper understanding of the Soviet Union by learning its customs, economy, history, and most of all, its language. Only Russian students were allowed to join.

1969

Auto Club. The following is the description of Auto Club in the 1969 Pinnacle: The driver nervously tugs at his gloves. The navigator, to the right of the driver, makes the last unnecessary yet impulsive check of his maps. The sound of the engine fills his ears, and he thinks of the road ahead. The Glenbard West Auto Club Road Rally is underway for these two. It will end only several hours later after a long, aggravating series of wrong turns and exhaustion. And most aggravating of all is the long flat stretch of pavement after the wrong turn at Hooterville. They lost as least 20 minutes on that unfortunate adventure. They had to get back to the main route and they had to do it fast.

1970

VICA: Vocational Industrial Club of America.

Distributive Education: Students competed in events such as sales presentation, public speaking, advertising, and Human Relations Case Problems.

Radio Glenbard: See more about WGHS in this book.

AFS: No description given.

Anglers: No description given. Fishing Club, most likely.

1971

Philosophy Club: The group studied and discussed the five main world religions: Christianity, Judaism, Islam, Hinduism, and Buddhism.

1972: Of special note, the Literary Society publishes "Early Wine," a literary magazine of student work.

1973 and 1974: No new clubs.

1975

Amazon Women Club: From the 1975 Pinnacle, Mr. Dick Nordmeyer had great faith in the so-called weaker sex when he agreed to sponsor a new club—the Amazon Women, whose theme was "Fight Fat with Fun." Specializing in the "fun" part of their theme, the Amazons invaded school with several new activities. First, they organized a party at Halloween, with girls trooping through school in costumes. That evening the Amazons when trick-or-treating in Glen Ellyn, collecting over 60 pounds of candy, which they gave to charity. Their first annual Amazon Bowl pitted the seniors against the juniors in a rugged game of touch football. The Amazons also held a legs contest.

1976
French Club (L'Alliance Fraincaise): Changes its name to French Fun and Food Club

1977
Health Occupations Club: Service to others was the aim of the Health Occupations Club. One of their projects was a party at Christmastime for the residents of the Manchester Nursing Home. They also raised $300 for the fight against muscular dystrophy.

1978 and 1979: No new clubs.

1980

S.U.P.E.R.: Students United to Promote Equal Rights encouraged an awareness for the need for equality.

Byzantium: The new, literary magazine is published. It featured the poems, art work, fiction, satire, and photos contributed by sixteen students. The title of the magazine was taken from the poem "Sailing to Byzantium," by William Butler Yeats. The city of Byzantium was thought to be the spiritual center of art. The event, Page to Stage, grew out of the submissions to Byzantium.

The Middle Earth Society: Stirred interest in the books of J.R.R. Tolkien. Part of a national organization, the 22-member organization met monthly to interpret the works of Tolkien. The group also sponsored several volleyball games.

1981 and 1982: No new clubs.

1983
Model U.N. is formed and participated in the 20th Annual North American Invitational Mode United Nations Convention in Washington D.C. Glenbard West's Model U.N. was the only delegation from Illinois.

1984, 1985, and 1986: No new clubs.

1987
Students for Students: In 1987, SfS holds a massive anti-substance abuse campaign. They begin Live Life Well Week.

1988
Youth and Governance Group: Sponsored by the Social Studies Department. This group learned about government first hand in after-school sessions by dedicating themselves to "grueling parliamentary procedure and bill-writing techniques."

1989
Target Success: As freshmen enter the halls of Glenbard West in the fall, they are not alone. The goal of two organizations, Target Success and Peer Groups, is to get the freshmen class involved in their new community, as well as learn something about themselves. Target Success is a support group which follows a "big brother/sister – little brother/sister" approach. The

big brothers/sisters are comprised of juniors and seniors who assist freshmen in the transition from junior high school. Peer Group help occurs when freshmen talk to student counselors who are juniors and seniors. They discuss a wide variety of subjects. The goal is to have the freshman obtain knowledge and also learn something about themselves.

1990: No new clubs

1991

ECO Club: The Environmental Concerns Organization (ECO). No description was given in the 1991 Pinnacle, but the 1992 edition states that ECO was originally created to celebrate Earth Day. In 1992, it began recycling cans and papers.

Students Against Homelessness: SAH became a prominent way in getting students to help the community. The club ran drives to collect food, toiletries, Christmas toys, and candy for Halloween. Members also donated the fund they raised to the "Apartment Project."

International Club: This club lets bilingual students, exchange students, and American students to get to know each other and share cultures. The members ate foods from cultures from all over the world, which brought the students closer and promoted wellbeing.

Improv Club: This was the new drama club at school. People could meet and work on their acting skills.

1992

Students for Students: This is an organization developed to promote the personal and social growth of its members and others. SFS sponsored Live Life Well Week and Exit with Pride. Members also organized an anti-substance abuse program geared to kindergarten through third grade students entitled "Don't Clown Around with Drugs." Clowns against Drugs are first formally mentioned in the 2002 Pinnacle. Target Success and Peer Group are part of SFS.

Amnesty International: This club was part of a world-wide organization that works to free political prisoners and preserve human rights. Members write letters and sign petitions to free unjustly accused prisoners. The club sold handmade bead necklaces as their fundraiser.

Intramural Hockey: This club offered students a chance to form their own teams.

Badminton Club: This club was created due to the popularity of the sport in gym classes.

Connect-Four Club: A club for those who enjoy board games.

1993

International Club: The purpose was to share cultures and interests with others—to promote cultural awareness and understanding.

Association of Concerned Teens: Known as A.C.T., this group formed an umbrella for three other groups: Students Against Homelessness, Amnesty International, and Direct Action. All three of these groups strove to expose students to all types of humanitarian action.

1994

The Flag Squad: The group had been active for many years prior, but in 1994 it was formally considered a club. While it still performed with the band, members no longer were required to be a member of the band itself.

The Foreign Language Club: In 1994, the three language classes (French, Spanish, German) all came together as one club. The club learned about each other's cultures and languages.

International Dance Troop: The group gathered on Wednesday evenings to learn and practice dances from around the world.

1995 and 1996: No new clubs.

1997

Scholastic Bowl: Schools compete against each other in a Jeopardy-like game. Just as in the TV game show, Jeopardy, the moderator asks questions, and the team who buzzes in first gets to answer the question.

1998

Investment Club: Students invest their own money to purchase stock and hopefully make a profit. At the end of 1998 school year, the club had over $8,000 in assets and more than 60 members.

1999

Science Olympiad: This science club competes in different events related to all areas of Science. A great description would be "a track meet of science events." Students might compete in general areas like Biology, Chemistry, and Physics or in specific areas such as astronomy or even bugs.

2000

Toadies: Although this group has been around for many years prior, it was in 2000 that they were recognized in Pinnacle. This group of technicians ran the lights and sound for all convos and school functions held in the auditorium. Years before this, the group had intended to be called The Roadies, but a typo put the letter "T" in the place of the "R"—since those two letters are next to each other on the keyboard. The result: The Toadies. The group of students liked Toadies more than Roadies, and the name stuck.

PRISM: This was a group started by students who want tolerance for all with a focus on gender issues and homophobia.

Saddle Club: This club started because of the group's affection for horses and their joy for riding.

Asian Club: This club gave students of any Asian background the opportunity to share their heritage and traditions.

Med Club: This club began because a group of advanced health students had an interest in medicine and careers related to medicine.

2001

Young Democrats: This group meets to inform and educate others about politics and democratic views and issues.

Tech Squad: This group of students was formed to pool the tech and computer knowledge of students to help teachers, classes, and students with their technical needs.

Latinos Unidos: The new name of the Spanish Club—also known as P.A.L.—The Pan American League. Latino Unidos celebrated the cultures of all Latin communities.

Steppers: No information given in 2001 Pinnacle. Only the group portrait was shown. Their picture is shown, at right.

2002

Breakdance Club: Students met after school to learn and practice breakdancing moves. The club also performed at the December 7, 2001 Pep Rally.

Simpsons Club: No information given in 2002 Pinnacle. Only a picture of the group was shown.

Club Ed: Similar to the Future Teachers of America, this club was new in 2002. FTA had stopped meeting years before Club Ed.

Glenbard Republicans: The goal of Glenbard Republicans is to educate members by discussing issues of the past and present, and to ensure a conservative viewpoint in school issues.

Societe Honoraire de Francais: French Honors Society. Students needed to have an A average in French for three semesters and a 4.50 GPA.

2003

Super Fans: A group of energetic and spirited students who are responsible for publicizing athletic events and getting other students to show up and be engaged in the event.

Anime Club: A group that allows diehard fans of anime to see some of the best animation and allows them to fully engage in an art form that many just saw as simply a trend.

2004

World Relief Club: This group focuses on their efforts to raise money to provide families in developing countries with animals that pave the way to self-reliance while also educating its members on current issues of third world countries.

2005

West Spirit: Promotes school spirit and good will at Glenbard West through their responsibility for decorations throughout the school and taking charge of holiday events.

2006: No new clubs.

2007
Multi-Cultural Club: Designated for students to get involved both in school and the community.

2008: No new clubs.

2009
SFPA: Students for the Protection of Animals. Students in the club volunteer at a local animal shelter. They also raise money for the care of animals. Participating in fundraisers (bake sale, jewelry party, and a garage sale) has allowed students to provide gifts to Willowbrook Wildlife Center and Oak Park Animal Shelter.

2010
Greenies (Recycling): Greenies allows students who care about the environment to help by taking out the schools recycling as well as offering extra credit to participants for certain science classes.

2011
JKB: (J. Kyle Braid) JKB leadership is a student athlete leadership organization which identifies and selects young adults who exhibit leadership potential, have a strong sense of moral values and possess the compassion necessary to improve the world.

2012
Dice it Up: This is a group for students who enjoy gaming away from the computer. They come to Dice It Up, bringing their favorite board games to play with other members.

Students for the Disabled Club asked, "Are you related to or friends with someone who is disabled? Do you have a disability yourself? Are you passionate about volunteering and making a difference in your school and the community? Then West Students for the Disabled is the club for you!"

Kids for a Cure: This club was created to raise awareness of and funding for those in our school community who were fighting/surviving cancer. It grew into awareness of other kinds of diseases that were challenging to cure or couldn't be cured at all like ALS and others. It was started by students whose siblings were fighting cancer and they needed a place to "fight" for them as a group.

Jam Club is a student driven organization where those who would like to play in a band with friends and others can participate in a fluid, loose, and creative atmosphere.

TV Broadcasting: Students came early in the morning to record the West Wind Announcements. They were later broadcast at the start of 2nd period.

Operation One World is a program designed to help English Language Learners (ELL students) as they transition into the Glenbard West community.

Ultimate Frisbee is a very competitive and exciting sport where you are constantly moving up and down the field. This year, we had a great turnout and because the weather was nice most of the year, we played many thrilling games.

Fashion Club: This is a club comprised of students who have a passion for fashion. The club's biggest event is an annual fashion show showcasing student style while putting money towards a good cause.

2013

Black Student Perspective (BSP): Changes to BSA (Black Student Association) in 2014. BSP is a club where students discussed issues at Glenbard West, from the perspective of the African-American student.

Rotary Interact Club: Rotary Interact is a branch of Rotary International at the high school level. It is an international service organization whose stated purpose is to bring together students within their school and community in order to provide humanitarian services, encourage high ethical standards in all vocation, and to advance goodwill and peace around the world.

Glenbard Global Giving: The club was designed to fund raise for a rotating major cause every year that was happening around the world. The club gave relief money to the hurricanes in Haiti, the earthquakes in Japan, and the Red Cross for storms in the US. The club also participated in Feed my Starving Children and other outreaches that came through the school—such as when the choir hosted kids from Uganda.

$100 Club: Later, this club became known as Project Action. This club's mission is to encourage philanthropic, entrepreneurial activity among students. The group/individual chooses a charity, plans the event and carries it out. There is the goal for one fundraiser for first semester and one for second semester. This way the students can focus on two big effective ones. The groups meet once a month and, as fundraisers approach, meet more frequently, and support one other with suggestions and ideas. Once they have completed the profit they made is sent to their chosen charity. This club believes this is a great way to give back to the community, give to a cause they are passionate about and learn what it takes to run a fundraiser. Students develop great leadership skills in this club.

Chinese Club: Made for any student interested in many aspects of the Chinese Culture. The club learns and gets a taste about Chinese festivals, fables, and major history of China.

2014

Yoga Club (shown at right) met once a week to work on flexibility, breathing techniques, and relaxation. Namaste.

Best Buddies at Glenbard West had its inaugural kick off in the fall of 2014. Best Buddies is an international organization, at Glenbard West, students with intellectual and developmental disabilities are paired with their neurotypical peers. The club's vision is inclusion for all and the club has added so much to the Glenbard community.

GLO: Glenbard Latino Organization

2015

WES: The Women Empowerment Society

STEM: Science Technology Engineering and Mathematics Club

MSA (Muslim Student Association) (shown at right): This is a group for Muslim students to spend time together. Students planned weekly activities for group members. It welcomed all students who wanted to participate.

2016
Political Science: Students gather to talk about political issues and policies.

2017: No new clubs.

Notable and Distinguished Alumni

The individuals that appear on the following pages have all attended Glenbard West High School. It is by no means an all-inclusive list. No committee picked these people for inclusion into this book. They have been "famous" and often talked about by students and teachers. They have their own page in Wikipedia. And so forth. A formal committee of teachers, administrators, and students have gathered in 2016-2017 to recognize distinguished alumni.

The inaugural class of Distinguished Alumni was honored on September 22, 2018. The following alumni were honored on that Homecoming weekend and their biographies can be found on the next few pages.

Mary Rohrs (1938)	**Lester Munson (1958)**	**Laurie Anderson (1965)**
Bruce Capel (1961)	**Bobby Rahal (1971)**	**Caryn Capotosto (1993)**
Nancy Derk Utley (1973)	**Thomas Gilardi (1986)**	

The second class of Distinguished Alumni was honored on September 28, 2019.

Joe Carlton (1946)	**Dr. John Clemens (1967)**	**Hollis Webster (1973)**	**"Chip" Hooper (1980)**
John Borg (1983)	**Jim Elliott (1987)**	**Sean Hayes (1988)**	**Maddi Bertrand (2018)**

Should you know of someone who should be included in this book,
please contact the sponsor of the GWHS History Society, Mr. Steven Wiersum.

steve_wiersum@glenbard.org

Class of 1935: Robert MacLeod

Robert MacLeod graduated from Glenbard High School in 1935. Playing football for Dartmouth College his coach, Earl "Red" Blaik called him "the greatest competitive athlete I've ever coached."

After college, he played two seasons with the Chicago Bears. He then served in the U.S. Marine Corps as a fighter pilot in World War II.

He left the service, highly decorated, as a Major in 1946. He entered the advertising and publishing business, became the publisher of Harper's Bazaar and vice-president and director of advertising for Hearst magazines.

In 1956, MacLeod became publisher and editorial director of Teen Magazine. The black and white photo of him on the beach in Malibu, California was taken for *Teen Magazine's* Great Model Search: 1984. In case you cannot find him, MacLeod is the one not wearing a swimsuit.

Class of 1938: Mary Rohrs: Distinguished Alumni Award class of 2018

Mary was one of the original graduating class of Glenbard West High School. Her first husband Art Johnston was shot down over France in 1944. Mary was a pregnant war widow (her first husband was shot down over France during WW2). In order to provide for herself and her new daughter she borrowed $1,500 and started the Mother Goose Shop. It became one of the largest and most respected independent children's clothing stores in the Chicagoland area.

Class of 1948*: Janice Rule
Actress, Dancer, Psychoanalyst.

*Janice would have graduated from Glenbard High School in 1948, left high school for Broadway after her Junior year.

Shown right, is a picture from her Junior year-- page 47 of the 1947 Pinnacle. She is simply identified as "Rule.")

According to Wiki, Janice Rule began dancing, at age 15, at Chez Paree, a Chicago nightclub known for its glamour. Several Glen Ellyn residents have related that Janice went into the city every day after school for either dance or singing lessons. Apparently, Janice

was also performing in the city at that time and would sit at a nightclub table and get help on her homework from the staff before the show began.

She also was a dancer in the 1949 Broadway production of Miss Liberty. She was pictured on the cover of Life magazine (January 8, 1951) as being someone to watch in the entertainment industry. Given a contract by Warner Bros., her first credited screen role was as Virginia in *Goodbye, My Fancy*, which featured Joan Crawford.

She appeared in *The Twilight Zone* season 1 episode, "Nightmare as a Child" as Helen Foley and in *Bell, Book and Candle*, which starred Kim Novak and Jimmy Stewart.

Class of 1956: Samuel Bodman

U.S. Secretary of Energy (2005—2009)

Samuel graduated from Cornell University and received his doctorate in chemical engineering from M.I.T. Later, he joined the faculty at M.I.T.

Dr. Bodman joined the George W. Bush administration during Bush's second term. As the Secretary of Energy, he was responsible for the country's nuclear weapons.

He died on September 7, 2018.

Class of 1956: Dick Pond

The following biography is used courtesy of his daughter, Kirsten Pond.

Dick was an All-State 880-yard runner (1956) from Glenbard West High School class of 1956, and an All-American in cross country (1960) at Western Michigan University. Dick taught history at GBW and coached XC and track for many years. It was during this time Dick realized his athletes did not have access to proper footwear. Dick then founded Dick Pond Athletics in 1969, in his family's garage in Glen Ellyn, IL. As the business grew, he began transporting shoes to schools and races in the back of his car.

Dick passed away at the age of 51 from Acute Leukemia. He is since an inducted member of the Western Michigan University Hall of Fame and The Independent Running Retailers Association Hall of Fame.

Today, Dick Pond Athletics, Inc. is still run by two of his five daughters (who all graduated from GBW) and has many retail stores and a national internet business. Dick's impact on athletes and runners was profound back then and continues as Dick Pond Athletics celebrates its 50th year in business. The company has enabled hundreds of thousands of people improve their lives through walking and running.

Class of 1958: Lester Munson
Distinguished Alumni Award class of 2018

After graduating from Glenbard, Lester attended Princeton University, where he served as editor of the Daily Princetonian, the school newspaper. He then received a law degree from the University of Chicago and practiced law in Chicago and

Wheaton until 1989 when he went back to his first love, sports journalism. He has worked at The National, Sports Illustrated, and ESPN and now does freelance investigative journalism.

He has made many guest appearances on sports radio and TV and is a frequent guest on WTTW Chicago Week in Review. He is also an adjunct professor at the Northwestern Medill School of Journalism.

For the last 12 years, Lester has been involved with the Hazelden Betty Ford Foundation. He works to fight addiction by "smashing the stigma of addiction", that is by educating on the disease of addiction, showing that people do recover from addiction, advocating for research and treatment funding.

He also served as a board member at an organization helping underprivileged youth in Chicago and volunteers his time freely by doing many speaking engagements in the community.

He has been the recipient of the University of Chicago Alumni Service Award for his long-time support and involvement at the University, has received national awards for his investigative journalism, and volunteers his time tirelessly, not only in the field of addiction but also with many community organizations and legal groups.

His friend, Susan Fox Gillis, wrote, "He is a credit to the Glenbard community. He remains proud of his varsity letter G (for basketball) although I don't think his letter jacket still fits!"

Class of 1964: Larry Shue

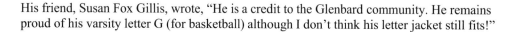

An actor and playwright, Larry wrote two often-performed plays, *The Foreigner* and *The Nerd*. Incidentally, *The Nerd*, starring Rowan Atkinson, became the top-grossing American play London's West End in 1986. (Source Wikipedia)

Larry perished in an aircraft crash in 1985. He was 39.

Class of 1965: Laurie Anderson: Distinguished Alumni Award class of 2018

Musician, songwriter, inventor, and performance artist. 2019 Grammy Award winner. *Landfall,* her Kronos Quartet collaboration, won Best Chamber Music/Small Music Ensemble Performance. She had been nominated three times previous to her 2019 award.

Shown, below, her 1965 senior portrait and as a sophomore cheerleader in the 1963 Pinnacle. She is the second from the left. In the *Pinnacle,* she is identified as Lauri Anderson.

Lauri Anderson

Class of 1967: Michael Herbick

Mike Herbick got his start in Ken Nordine's studio in Chicago. According to IMDb, he has nearly 100 movie credits to his name, including *Lord of the Flies, Teenage Mutant Ninja Turtles, The Shawshank Redemption, Batman Forever, Phenomenon, Small Soldiers, Star Trek: Insurrection, Analyze This, Three Kings, The Green Mile, Training Day, The Replacements,* and *Valkyrie.*

He is an Oscar nominated sound mixer and has won an Emmy for his work on *Lonesome Dove*. He also is a British Academy Award winner for his work on *The Fugitive*.

Class of 1968: Dianne Holum

Won Olympic Silver and Bronze medals in 1968 and Gold and Silver medals in 1972 at the Winter Olympics in speed skating. According to ABC News, Dianne "won more medals than any U.S. woman in Winter Games history and captured gold in Munich in 1972.

Not pictured in 1968 *Pinnacle*.

At left, the picture used on Dianne Holum's Wikipedia page.

Class of 1968: Jeffery Deaver

Mystery author, recently chosen to be the new author of the James Bond novels, is perhaps best known for his creation of the character Lincoln Rhyme in novels such as The Bone Collector, which was also made into a major motion picture starring Angelina Jolie.

Below is a list of his books, according to his website, JeffreyDeaver.com

The Never Game (Coming May 2019) The Cutting Edge (2018) The Burial Hour (2017) The Steel Kiss (2016) Solitude Creek (2015) The Skin Collector (2014) The October List (2013) The Kill Room (2013) XO (2012) Carte Blanche (2011) Edge (2010) The Burning Wire (2010) Roadside Crosses (2009) The Bodies Left Behind (2008) The Broken Window (2008) The Sleeping Doll (2007) The Cold Moon (2006) The Twelfth Card (2005) Garden of Beasts (2004) The Vanished Man (2003) The Stone Monkey (2002) The Blue Nowhere (2001) Hell's Kitchen (2001) Speaking In Tongues (2000) The Empty Chair (2000) The Devil's Teardrop (1999) The Coffin Dancer (1998) The Bone Collector (1997) A Maiden's Grave (1995) Praying For Sleep (1994) The Lesson of Her Death (1993) Bloody River Blues (1993) Mistress of Justice (1992) Shallow Graves (1992) Hard News (1991) Death of a Blue Movie Star (1990) Manhattan is My Beat (1988)

The Lincoln Rhyme Series
The Cutting Edge (2018) The Burial Hour (2017) The Steel Kiss (2016) The Skin Collector (2014) The Kill Room (2013) XO (2012) small appearance The Burning Wire (2010) The Broken Window (2008) The Cold Moon (2006) The Twelfth Card (2005) The Vanished Man (2003) The Stone Monkey (2002) The Empty Chair (2000) The Coffin Dancer (1998) The Bone Collector (1997) The Colter Shaw Series The Never Game (Coming May 2019)

The Kathryn Dance
Series Solitude Creek (2015) XO (2012) The Burning Wire (2010) (appearance) Roadside Crosses (2009) The Sleeping Doll (2007) The Cold Moon (2006) (appearance) The Rune Series Hard News (1991) Death of a Blue Movie Star (1990) Manhattan is My Beat (1988)

The John Pellam Series
Hell's Kitchen (2001) Bloody River Blues (1993) Shallow Graves (1992)

Class of 1969: Linda Lynch Kurzawa

From the Leonard Memorial Home obituary, October 14, 2018

Linda Alice Kurzawa, 66, a longtime resident of Winfield, Illinois, passed away surrounded by her family on October 14, 2018 following a brave battle with cancer. She was born October 16, 1951 to William and Lois Lynch of Glen Ellyn, Illinois. She was a graduate of Glenbard West High School where she met her husband Dennis of 46 years. The two married on September 16, 1972.

Linda had a servant's heart. She devoted more than three decades to improving the quality of life of the residents of DuPage County. Linda served on the county board from 1992 – 2010. During this time, she also served as a forest preserve commissioner. She was appointed to the DuPage County Board of Health, where she served as board president until her time of death. The professional achievement of which she was most proud was the building of the behavioral health community center that is named in her honor.

Class of 1969: Kenneth Popejoy

Ken epitomizes the idea of a scholar-athlete. An incredible athlete, Ken ran in the high school national meet in 1969, finishing second to Steve Prefontaine. As a Hilltopper, he finished in the top 6% of class, was inducted into the NHS, became a State Cross Country champion and the State mile champion, and was named a National High School All-American athlete.

His Glenbard West success carried over to his life post-Glenbard. As a student at Michigan State University in 1973, Ken ran a World Record five consecutive, sub-four minute mile races, becoming a Big Ten and NCAA Mile champion. He graduated with honors.

In 1975, while attending law school, he was ranked 9th in the world in the 1,500 and mile race. He served as a coach, co-coaching Jim Spivey, winner of the 1987 Bronze Medal in the World Championships. Ken won the World Masters Mile Championship in Turku, Finland in 1991. He is listed in both the Chicagoland and the Michigan State Sports Hall of Fame.

He earned his J.D. from Kent College of Law, graduating with honors. He worked as an attorney and has served as an Acting Chief Judge. He is currently serving as a Circuit Judge for the 18th Judicial Court.

Attended 1970 and 1971: Gary Sinise

While actor, writer, musician Gary Sinise did not graduate from Glenbard West (he would have been in the 1973 graduating class), he did attend the high school for his first two years.

From Wikipedia: Among other awards, he has won an Emmy Award, a Golden Globe Award, a star on Hollywood Walk of Fame and has been nominated for an Academy Award.

Sinise is known for several memorable roles. These include George Milton in *Of Mice and Men*, Lieutenant Dan Taylor in *Forrest Gump* (for which he was nominated for the Academy Award for Best Supporting Actor), Harry S. Truman in *Truman* (for which he won a Golden Globe), Ken Mattingly in *Apollo 13*, Detective Jimmy Shaker in *Ransom*, Detective Mac Taylor in the CBS *series CSI: NY* (2004–13), and George C. Wallace in the television film *George Wallace* (for which he won an Emmy). From 2016 to 2017, Sinise starred as Special Agent Jack Garrett in *Criminal Minds: Beyond Borders*.

Photo by Blake Little, used with permission

Above, Gary Sinise in the 1970 *Pinnacle*

Class of 1970: Ted Wass

After Glenbard West, Ted graduated from Goodman School of Drama in Chicago. He then went on to enjoy a Broadway career, playing the character of Danny Zuko in *Grease*. He also performed in the Broadway musical *They're Playing our Song*. Ted then launched a TV and film career with appearances in *Curse of the Pink Panther, Oh God You Devil,* and *The Longshot*.

Perhaps his most well-known role was that of Danny in *Soap*. He also appeared in *Blossom*. Ted has also had a career in directing—becoming one of the best multi-camera directors in the industry.

His directing credits include episodes for *Big Bang Theory, Less Than Perfect, Crumbs, Two and a Half Men, Everybody Hates Chris, Brothers, Melissa & Joey, 2 Broke Girls, Rule of Engagement, Last Man Standing, Mom,* and *Cristela*. Ted was also the producer for 12 episodes of *Brothers*. (source IMDb)

Class of 1971: Julie Reece Deaver

She is the author of several novels, including *Say Goodnight, Gracie*, an ALA Best Book for Young Adults, which introduced two of the characters featured in *The Night I Disappeared*. Deaver has worked as a teacher's aide in special education and started her writing career in television comedy.

She is an artist as well as a writer; her illustrations have appeared in *The New Yorker, Reader's Digest*, and the *Chicago Tribune*. She lives on the Monterey Peninsula in California with her blue-eyed cat, Lincoln Rhyme. (Text from Simon & Schuster website)

Class of 1971: Susan Lloyd

Susan was the executive director of the Zilber Family Foundation, a private Milwaukee-based foundation. According to its website, the Zilber Family Foundation, "is dedicated to enhancing the well-being of individuals, families, and neighborhoods."

Class of 1971: Bobby Rahal
Distinguished Alumni Award class of 2018

Bobby Rahal is an American former auto racing driver and team owner. As a driver he won three championships and 24 races in the CART open-wheel series, including the 1986 Indianapolis 500. He also won the 2004 Indianapolis 500 as a team owner for the winning driver, Buddy Rice.

After retiring as a driver, Rahal held managerial positions with the Jaguar Formula 1 team and also was an interim president of the CART series. Rahal was also a sports car driver during the 1980s and made one NASCAR start for the Wood Brothers.

In 1986, Rahal dramatically passed Kevin Cogan on a restart with two laps to go to win the Indianapolis 500, only days before his team owner, Jim Trueman died of cancer. Later that year, Rahal won his first CART championship, and successfully defended it the following year. In 1996, talk show host David Letterman became a minority owner with Bobby in 1996. The team became known as Team Rahal in 1996 and Rahal Letterman Racing in 2004.

At WeatherTech Raceway Laguna Seca, the back straight leading up to the corkscrew was named the "Rahal Straight" in his honor. His awards include induction into the International Motorsports Hall of Fame, the Motorsports Hall of Fame of America, the Sports Car Club of America Hall of Fame, and the Indianapolis Motor Speedway Museum Auto Racing Hall of Fame.

Class of 1971: Tom LaPorte

Tom began using his journalistic talent writing articles for The Glen Bard—the GWHS school newspaper. He was still in high school when he interviewed social activist Abbie Hoffman, a man on the FBI's Most Wanted list. Tom later pursued a career in journalism. In addition to journalism, he became the Assistant Water Commissioner for the City of Chicago.

Left, Tom and fellow reporter John Fenoglio working on a 5 pm news broadcast for BMIR. Photo by: dimitre.com ©2007. Used with permission.

One way he distinguished himself was by reducing the number of manhole covers being stolen. His solution: to have the manhole covers blessed by a priest. He invited the media to report on the blessing of the covers which greatly reduced the number of thefts. He also taught at Columbia University. Tom has also been called "A major force of the Burning Man festival," working there since 2005. He helped create the radio station BMIR (Burning Man Informational Radio 94.5 FM and became The Voice of the Burn. Said John Fenoglio, pictured above and a reporter at KTLA, "Tom had a way of walking into a room and knowing everybody. He was great at putting ideas together and putting people together."

Class of 1973: Nancy Derk (Jacobs)
Distinguished Alumni Award class of 2018

A movie studio executive known as Nancy Utley, she was publicly thanked during the 87th Academy Awards (Oscars) in 2015 when *Birdman* won best picture. She was also mentioned in an acceptance speech in 2018 at the 90th Academy Awards.

She is the President, Fox Searchlight / VP, AMPAS: Fox Searchlight, Fox Searchlight, Academy of Motion Picture Arts & Sciences.

Releases include *The Favourite, The Shape of Water, Far from the Madding Crowd, Me and Earl and the Dying Girl, Brooklyn, He Named Me Malala, Birdman, Wild, 12 Years a Slave, The Grand Budapest Hotel, Beasts of the Southern Wild, The Best Exotic Marigold Hotel, The Descendants, The Tree of Life, Black Swan, 127 Hours, Crazy Heart, 500 Days of Summer, Slumdog Millionaire, The Wrestler, Juno, Once, Little Miss Sunshine, The Last King of Scotland, Sideways* and *Napoleon Dynamite.*

At right, Nancy's picture as a National Merit Semi Finalist. Also, above left, wearing the checkered dress, Nancy (president of the Forerunners Club), helps a gentleman find his reserved seat at the Choir's Christmas Concert. (From the 1973 *Pinnacle*.)

Class of 1973: Jim Molinari

A basketball coach and lawyer, Jim is an assistant coach at Nebraska. Previously, he was the men's head basketball coach at Western Illinois University. He has also enjoyed coaching capacities at Ball State University, University of Minnesota, Northern Illinois University, and Bradley University. He also scouted for the Toronto Raptors and the Miami Heat.

Class of 1973: Jim Lentz

Jim Lentz is chief executive officer of Toyota Motor North America, and an operating officer of parent company Toyota Motor Corporation located in Japan. He is past chairman of the American Automotive Alliance, and currently serves on Daniels College of Business at the University of Denver executive advisory board, The Dallas Stars ownership advisory group, and is appointed as board member to the Texas Economic Development Corporation.

Notable awards include: Advertising age Marketer of the year 2006, Industry leader of the year by the Automotive Hall of Fame in 2014, Leon Higgin Botham leadership award in 2015, D magazine CEO of the year in 2018. Lentz earned a BSBA and an MBA-Finance from the University of Denver. Honorary doctorate degrees from Northwood University and the University of Denver. Lives in Westlake Texas with his wife Barbara.

Class of 1975: Tim Derk

Tim Derk has been a part of the Spurs organization for more than 30 years. He is the creator of the Spurs Coyote mascot and performed as the Coyote for over 21 years. During this time, he entertained fans at 992 consecutive home Spurs games and made over 5000 public appearances. In 2007, the Coyote was elected to the Mascot Hall of Fame.

Tim received a Lifetime Achievement Award from the NBA, as well as being nominated for the San Antonio Sports Hall of Fame in 2016. He has written a book entitled "Hi Mom, Send Sheep" about his experiences behind the mask and his outlook on life. The book is currently available online at Amazon.com.

In his present role, Tim manages and recruits for the Spurs office of Service Innovation. He also teaches specialized customer service.

Tim is also the inventor of the T-Shirt Cannon. According to a June 2013 New York Times article written by Pagan Kennedy, "It weighed 90 pounds, including the tanks," says Tim Derk of the T-shirt cannon he helped invent when he worked as the Coyote mascot for the San Antonio Spurs in the 1990s. "It was like carrying a TV set on your back. The gun was probably at least four feet long. It used a cast-iron pipe — the kind that goes into the floor underneath your commode. It just weighed a ton."

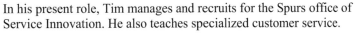

Class of 1975: Patricia Tallman

Actress and stuntwoman, Patricia Tallman is perhaps best known for her work in the 1990 cult classic *Night of The Living Dead* as Barbara, the beleaguered heroine. Some may argue she is best known for her role as Lyta Alexander in the Hugo Award winning series, *Babylon 5*. Either way, she has been swept into a career that features horror and Science Fiction projects.

She is less recognizable, but no less memorable, as the Horror Hag in *Evil Dead III, Army of Darkness*. As a stuntwoman, Pat has taken the fall for Laura Dern in *Jurassic Park*, Geena Davis in *Long Kiss Goodnight*, Robin Wright in *Forrest Gump* and hundreds of others.

Fans make a game of spotting her in the over 50 appearances in the Star Trek franchises: *The Next Generation*, *Deep Space Nine* and *Voyager* as well as the feature film *Generations*.

She has been leading people on epic quests to live their dreams of adventure, check her site www.QuestRetreats.com for the next adventures!

Class of 1976: H. Gordon Boos

From the April 12, 2004 *Variety* article:

Born in Glen Ellyn, Boos become a leading assistant director after moving to L.A. He worked with directors including Francis Coppola, Oliver Stone, Norman Jewison and Ron Shelton.

Among his credits as assistant director are *Valley Girl, The Rookie, Tin Cup, The Godfather: Part III* and *Platoon*.

Boos was twice nominated for DGA honors and was part of the crew for Oliver Stone's 1986 win for *Platoon*. He also assistant directed over 100 commercials and music videos. Boos directed four feature films: *The Vivero Letter, Perfect Assassins, Touch Me* and *Red Surf*. In addition, Gordon had writing credits on *Touch Me* and *Red Surf*.

Pictured left, his 1975 yearbook senior photo.

Pictured at right, H. Gordon Boos plays George in *Our Town*. The Glen Theater also has a plaque about him in the lobby.

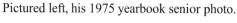

Class of 1978: Erin Clark

From the KSBW website:

Prior to her arrival at KSBW in 1998, Erin worked for more than a decade at our Hearst Television Inc sister station, WPTZ-TV in Plattsburg, New York. She grew up in suburban Chicago and graduated from the University of Vermont.

Erin actively supports various nonprofit projects across the Central Coast. She is the proud mother of two and resides in Carmel.

Class of 1979: Peter Roskam

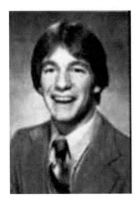

U. S. Congressman, representing Illinois's 6th congressional district (2007—2018)

Class of 1979: Brian Markinson

According to IMDB: "Brian Markinson is an actor, known for *Shooter* (2007), *Continuum* (2012) and *The Curse of the Jade Scorpion* (2001). Graduated from New York's American Academy of Dramatic Arts in 1983."

He also appeared in *Mad Men* as Dr. Arnold Rosen.

Class of 1980: Philip M. Krupp

An independent television and motion picture producer. While acknowledging his years making movies with Erickson Artists Productions in Glen Ellyn (starting at Churchill School and continuing through Glenbard West High School), it wasn't until after he moved to Los Angeles in 1985 that he gained a foothold in the entertainment industry at Braun Entertainment Group, where he worked in development and production. During that time, he sold, developed and produced numerous television series, mini-series, movies for television and feature films. Among his credits are the GLAAD Award winning television movie, *A Girl Like Me: The Gwen Arajuo Story,* the Christopher Award winning television movie, *The Gabby Douglas Story* and the acclaimed independent feature, *Edges of the Lord.* Krupp received a Bachelor of Science degree in Broadcast Journalism from the University of Illinois at Champaign-Urbana, and resides with his family in Los Angeles, California.

Class of 1980: Ralph S. Covert

Two Jeff Awards for playwriting. Grammy nominated musician. The leader of the of children's music group Ralph's World, featured on the Disney Channel, Ralph is also the lead singer and songwriter of the Chicago-based indie rock band, The Bad Examples. He has toured the world playing music, including at festivals like Lollapalooza, Ravinia, and Austin City Limits. Working with G Riley Mills, he has written numerous plays and musicals, including *Sawdust and Spangles* and *Streeterville*, both of which won the Joseph Jefferson Citation for Best New Work. Their musical *Hundred Dresses* has been produced many times nationwide, include off-Broadway in New York.

Class of 1980: Donald "Chip" Hooper

Chip honed his skills as a photographer to some degree by providing some amazing photographs for Glenbard West football programs that Guy and Sharon Matthew put together—as part of the GW Boosters—in the 1970's. They have fond memories of his rushing the first developed films, printed on contact sheets from a Saturday game in order to select shots for the next game's program. He worked to make his photos unique and fun which became real crowd pleasers. Students would buy the programs in order to see if they were photographed and pictured in the "Were you There?" page of photos. If your photo was circled, you would win a prize and it was all the talk that week in school!

Chip was also well known for his work with Phish and Dave Matthews Band, the famed artist agent was revered across the music industry. In later years Chip said that his photography gave him hours of pleasure in an attempt to find a satisfying downtime from the busy music world he had established for himself.

Chip died after a long battle with cancer. He was 53. As Patrick Jordan wrote in Hooper's *Relix* obituary, "Chip's passions for music, art, friends and, especially, his family were incredibly contagious to anyone he came in contact with, and he was beloved for it."

Class of 1981: Fareed Haque

Guitarist and professor of Jazz and Classical Guitar Studies at Northern Illinois University. He was called the "best world guitarist" by *Guitar Player* magazine, 2009. At right, Fareed at 2018 JazzFest. Photo by Claudia Finley. Used with permission.

From his website: Fareed Haque is a modern guitar virtuoso. Since 2011, Haque has returned to his first loves, jazz guitar and classical guitar. He has been busy performing and recording with his trio featuring legendary B3 virtuoso Tony Monaco, his own trio and jazz quartet, as well as his larger world music group the Flat Earth Ensemble.

Recent releases include the critically acclaimed Out of Nowhere featuring drummer Billy Hart and bassist George Mraz, The Flat Earth Ensemble's latest release Trance Hypothesis, and The Tony Monaco/Fareed Haque release Furry Slippers that reached the top 10 in Jazz Radio Airplay.

IN addition, Fareed has performed at the Chicago, Detroit, and Java Jazz festivals and was featured as part of the Made in Chicago Series performing with his numerous groups at Millennium Park's Pritzker Pavilion in Chicago. He also performed and arranged numerous classical programs as 2013 artist-in-residence for The Chicago Latin Music Festival, was featured on WBEZ, as well as WFMT's Fiesta! radio programs, and has recorded his arrangement of Piazzolla's 5 Tango Sensations, El Alevin by Eduardo Angulo Leo Brouwer's Quintet for Guitar and String Quartet with the critically acclaimed Kaia String Quartet. Haque continues to tour and record extensively along with documenting his unique teaching methods in a series of best-selling interactive video courses through TrueFire.

Class of 1982: John Borg

John Borg has developed and designed some of the most popular pinball machines to date. In 2018, he released *The Munsters* pinball machine. He has presented at the Texas Pinball Festival, one of the largest pinball festivals in the world.

At right, John holds a giant baseball bat with Butch Patrick, the actor who portrayed Eddie Munster on *The Munsters*. One of his vendors made oversized baseball bats like the one Eddie held in the opening credits of *The Munsters* show.

Class of 1982: Jo Bennett

After graduating in 1982 Jo Bennett was discovered by a model scout and moved to Europe to begin an international career that is still ongoing today in 2019. She experimented living in different fashion capitals (London, Milan, Munich, and New York), but chose Paris as her base and worked worldwide for dozens of magazines, hundreds of advertising campaigns, fashion catalogs, and appeared in over 40 television commercials.

Some of her latest work from the 2000's can be seen on her site www.jobennett.co, the highlights from the 80's and 90's on her Facebook page, and several commercials on YouTube. Through modeling she travelled to over 25 countries, rubbed shoulders with celebrities and influencers, and speaks fluent French.

A quote from a captioned photo of hers:

"Defining 'beauty' is a never-ending debate. We are all born beautiful, but our culture has this need to establish standards to define who is to be considered 'beautiful'. I recently celebrated 30 happy years of modeling and want you to know that I recognize I owe my success to you. According to society's criteria I was born with the right face, in the right place, at the right time. And I just want to express thanks, with all my heart.

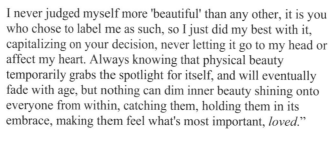

I never judged myself more 'beautiful' than any other, it is you who chose to label me as such, so I just did my best with it, capitalizing on your decision, never letting it go to my head or affect my heart. Always knowing that physical beauty temporarily grabs the spotlight for itself, and will eventually fade with age, but nothing can dim inner beauty shining onto everyone from within, catching them, holding them in its embrace, making them feel what's most important, *loved*."

Jo is an advocate for less photo retouching in the media and hopes through her images to promote 'positive ageing', inspire women to consider self-love and self-care a priority and to know that beauty has no expiration date when it comes from within.

Her dream since the age of 17 was to live in the Caribbean. Today, married with two children, she lives on the French West Indian island Guadeloupe, is the founder and owner of an oceanfront vacation rental complex, and travels to Europe for bookings.

Class of 1983: Tom Hodges

At left, Tom's sophomore yearbook picture (1981 *Pinnacle).*

Tom Hodges is an actor, producer and director who attended Glenbard West as part of the class of 1983. His acting career started with *Lucas* (he played the character of Bruno), followed by roles in *Steel Magnolias, Revenge of the Nerds II, Heavyweights,* and several other films and TV shows.

He has directed and produced numerous short films which have collectively garnered more than thirty festival awards and led to his selection by *Filmmaker Magazine* as one of their "25 New Faces of Indie." His short film "Last Request" sold to HBO and was selected as one of the ten semifinalists for the 2001 Academy Awards.

Hodges has been partnered with David Schwimmer in the production company Dark Harbor Stories for the past 19 years. Together they have developed and produced several plays, television projects and features. Most notable is the 2011 indie film "Trust," starring Clive Owen, Viola Davis, Jason Clarke, and Katherine Keener.

Class of 1983: Sarah Powers-Barnhard

Sarah started her volleyball career being named a *Tribune* All Stater in November 1982. She was an integral person who helped lead the GBW girls' volleyball team downstate in 1981 and 1982. She earned a scholarship to Division 1, Western Michigan. Sarah was named First Team All-MAC 1984-85 and was an All American in 1985, that summer Sarah was asked to represent the USA traveling to Japan and China to compete. Sarah graduated WMU with school records for kills (1,387), digs (964), and points (1725.5), and her total of 173 career service aces still stands as the school record. In 1997 was inducted into the WMU Athletic Hall of Fame.

From 1987-1989 Sarah Played professionally for the Major League Volleyball Association's Chicago Breeze. Sarah was inducted into the Mid-American Conference Hall of Fame (June 2016) as the first volleyball player to be inducted.

Sarah presently runs Powers Volleyball Club out of Jacksonville, Florida and she is still involved in running youth volleyball clinics in the Glen Ellyn area.

Class of 1984: Nancy Reno

Olympic competitor in beach volleyball (1996). Nancy won a bronze medal at the 1997 Beach Volleyball World Championships.

Pictured at right, Nancy Reno and May Smith block a shot.

Class of 1984: Phil Vischer

Author, actor, and puppeteer. Phil Vischer co-founded Veggie Tales.

Class of 1986: Thomas Gilardi
Distinguished Alumni Award class of 2018

During his time at Glenbard West, Tom was the Captain of football team his senior year, a Member of Hitters Club, and an All-State football player.

He received his B.A. from Holy Cross and his M.S. in Social Work from Loyola University of Chicago

He has more than 25 years in leadership positions at one of the largest orphanages in the U.S. that has touched the lives of more than 30,000 kids since 1887.

Tom personifies what Glenbard West teachers and athletic coaches strive to instill in students - do what you love, love what you do, and make an impact in life. In other words, be inspiring. Inspire others. Inspire others to do great things.

After Glenbard West, Tom went on to Holy Cross - following in the footsteps of the Detmer brothers - and played football while earning a first-rate college degree.

As his brother, John, wrote in his nomination, "After college, Tom followed what he thought was the career path that others wanted for him. That meant moving to Los Angeles to work in banking at what is now Wells Fargo.

But Tom listened to his heart, mind and soul, telling his parents that he wanted to be a social worker.

Even better, Tom decided to enter into social work as a volunteer with the Jesuit Volunteer Corp in Milwaukee. That experience solidified his resolve and love for others - and above all wanting to give back, especially to those most in need. Tom went on to earn a master's degree in Social Work at Loyola University of Chicago, while also starting to work at Mercy Boys and Girls Home.

During the more than 25 years at Mercy, where he has risen through the ranks to become the Chief Operating Officer of this organization, he has touched the lives of hundreds - if not thousands - of kids in Chicago that desperately needed help.

He and his wife, Kara, who is a regional director for the March of Dimes, have two kids - Katherine and Jack.

Class of 1986: Amy Carlson

An actress who works in film and television, Amy plays Alex Taylor on the TV series *Third Watch*, Linda Reagan on *Blue Bloods*, and Kelly Gaffney on *Law & Order: Trial by Jury*. She has many movie credits to her name including *Green Lantern, Anamorph,* and *Natural Selection*. She was nominated for Outstanding Female Newcomer in the 1995 Soap Opera Digest Awards and for a Daytime Emmy Award for supporting actress in 1998. According to TVGuide.com, she hopes one day to ride a motorcycle across Vietnam.

Class of 1986: Joel Jeske

Three-time New York Drama Desk Award Nominee and a writer and actor, Joel Jeske has been a professional clown, writer, and director for 25 years performing nationally, internationally, in New York City. He has written and created comedy material for Ringling Bros & Barnum and Bailey Circus, Cirque du Soleil, and New York's Big Apple Circus. He has also worked for 17 years in New York and Connecticut hospitals on staff as clown doctor: Dr. Yadontsay for Big Apple Circus Clown Care Unit and the national hospital program Healthy Humor. For 14 years, Joel has been the Associate Artistic Director of Parallel Exit, a New York based theater company.

 Joel created and starred in two productions for the Big Apple Circus in 2015 and 2017. A graduate of Ringling Bros and Barnum and Bailey Clown College in 1996, Joel toured with Ringling Bros., Cirque du Soleil, and Big Apple Circus for over a decade. Most recently, Joel was the movement and physical comedy consultant on *SpongeBob SquarePants: The Musical*. In Chicago, he worked in television production as a writer and associate producer, has performed with both the Second City and ImprovOlympic, and created the theatrical sub-genre of "Clown Theater" for the Chicago Theater Scene before touring with Ringling Bros. in 1996.

Class of 1986: Christina Filiaggi

Radio producer and on-air talent.

Class of 1988: Rob Boras

From Wiki, " American football coach who is the tight ends coach of the Buffalo Bills of the National Football League (NFL). He served as offensive coordinator of the St. Louis/Los Angeles Rams from 2015–2016 and as head coach at Benedictine University in 1998. During his career, he has also been an assistant coach at DePauw, Texas, UNLV, as well as for the NFL's Chicago Bears and Jacksonville Jaguars."

Class of 1988: Sean Hayes

Emmy Award-winning actor, best known for his role as Jack McFarland on the television series *Will & Grace.* At right, a 2018 picture of Sean with Glenbard West principal, Dr. Peter Monaghan. Sean had stopped by Glenbard West for a surprise visit. He even stopped by one of the theater classes to say hello.

According to his *Wikipedia* page, Sean won a Primetime Emmy Award, four SAG Awards, and one American Comedy Award. He has also earned six Golden Globe nominations. He runs a production company called Hazy Mills Productions. Finally, for his work on Broadway, he received a Tony Award for Best Performance by a Leading Actor in a Musical.

Class of 1990: Nina Bargiel

First and foremost, Nina is a TV writer. She has written for such shows as *Lizzie McGuire*, *Grim Adventures of Billy & Mandy*, *Barbie*, and *DC Superhero Girls*. She also writes for Nickelodeon, Disney Channel, Titmouse and Netflix.

But wait! There's more! When she is not typing away, she also is a TV talking head, appearing on BBCa and CoziTV.

Finally, Nina is a two-time Emmy nominee. (Which means she is a two-time Emmy loser*.)

Nina's words! Do NOT send hate mail to the editor!

Class of 1993: Caryn Capotosto: Distinguished Alumni Award class of 2018

Caryn is an established documentary film producer with multiple academy credits to her name. Her body of work covers a fantastic depth of topics which otherwise would be overlooked. She has produced 14 different works and has won multiple awards. Her bodies of work tell the deep story of media of individuals. She is head of productions at Tremolo Productions.

Caryn has a BA from Columbia College with a focus on photography and an MA from the University of Chicago. In fact, we were told that she also took a photography class at Glenbard West.

Photo by Alicia Rose

Her latest documentary, *Won't You Be My Neighbor?* is feature documentary about Mister Rogers that was an official selection of the 2018 Sundance Film Festival and was released theatrically in June 2018--including our favorite Glen Ellyn Theater, The Glen.

Caryn received a 2016 News and Documentary Emmy Award for her role as Co-Producer on Best of Enemies, and was the Associate Producer on the Academy Award and Grammy Award-winning documentary, *20 Feet from Stardom*, a film about the lives of the backup singers who have performed behind music legends like the Rolling Stones, Bette Midler and Bruce Springsteen.

Her other feature documentaries include Crossfire Hurricane an HBO show and the documentary series *Abstract: The Art of Design* for Netflix.

Her work has been called, "an inspiration."

Caryn was nominated by her friend, Rajesh Singh, who is also a Glenbard West and District 41 schools' alum. According to Rajesh, "Her documentaries are a reflection of her transparency and honesty and are grounded in the world around us."

Class of 1994: Becky Sundstrom

Competed in the 1998 and 2002 Winter Olympic Games as a member of the US Speedskating Team in the 500 meter, 1000 meter and 1500 meter events. Her best finish was 6th place in the women's 1000m event in 1998. Other career highlights include winning the Jr. World Championships in 1995, setting two Junior World Records, winning three World Cup medals in the 1000 meters, two bronze and one silver, and finishing 5th in the overall World Cup classification in the 1000m.

Becky also took a brief break from working in her family's development/home construction business to consult for NBC during the 2006 Winter Olympic Games in Torino, Italy as a "spotter" on the production team.

Class of 1995: Zak Bagans

The lead investigator in Travel Channel TV show *Ghost Adventures*

Class of 1995: Matt Bowen

NFL defensive back (2000—06). He played for the St. Louis Rams, Green Bay Packers, Washington Redskins, and the Buffalo Bills.

He also contributed to the *Chicago Tribune* as a sports writer.
He is currently an analyst for ESPN.

Class of 1998: Erin Gilreath

Erin was NCAA champion in 2003 in the 20# weight throw while competing at the University of Florida. She also held the world best in the 20# weight throw and was the first woman in the event to eclipse an 80' throw.

Erin held the American Record in the hammer throw for over 7 years and was on the World Championship team for the hammer throw in 2005 (Helsinki) and 2009 (Berlin).

She is a five-time US Champion.

Class of 1999: Molly Worthen

Molly Worthen is a historian of American religion and a liberal journalist. She is assistant professor of history at the University of North Carolina at Chapel Hill.

She has authored several books and is a contributing Op-Ed writer for *The New York Times*.

Photo by Jafar Fallahi

Class of 2000: Mike Hall

Mike Hall graduated from Glenbard West in 2000, and from the University of Missouri in 2004. He was the winner of ESPN's 'Dream Job' and with that his sportscasting career began as a 'SportsCenter' anchor. In 2005 he became the first Signature Host on ESPN's national college sports network, ESPNU. Mike moved back home to Chicago to launch another college sports network, the Big Ten Network, in 2007. He has been there ever since hosting football and men's basketball pregame, halftime, and postgame studio shows. He also has done sideline reporting for the NFL on FOX, and the Big Ten Men's Basketball Tournament.

Class of 2003: Katie Visco

In 2009, promoting the importance of a bold and passion-driven life, Katie ran solo across America, from Boston to San Diego, and became the 2nd youngest and 13th woman overall to make the crossing. During, and the year after her transAmerican crossing, she raised funds for the charity, Girls on the Run, and also stopped to visit more than two hundred audiences en route to spread her message to young and old alike. Running has been a versatile cornerstone of her wellbeing for years, and she especially loves the trails!

Katie also has 10+ years of experience as a community-builder and entrepreneur. She has started eight businesses and campaigns and is currently the proud owner and soup maestra behind Hot Love Soup, a soup and bone broth delivery company in Austin, Texas and now also in Missoula, Montana. She is a 2007 Economics graduate of Carleton College in Northfield, Minnesota.

Visco lives and works to see courage, community, and true connection happen in this world. Besides trail running, biking, creating delicious food, and traveling, Katie loves her husband and family very much and enjoys getting to hear the stories of others. She's been writing since she was six and hopes to publish a book one day. She loves sharing her journeys with others in hopes of inspiring growth, courage, curiosity and joy.

Find Katie: Instagram @katievisco and on the web: katievisco.com and hotlovesoup.com

Class of 2004: Peter Rahal and Jared Smith

After graduating from Glenbard West High School, Peter and Jared created RX Bars: a high-protein snack bar Cooking and creating them in the kitchen of Peter's parents' house, they soon began making over 1,000 bars a week.

They began making the bars in 2012 and quickly sold the bars at gyms and fitness centers. In 2017, RX Bars were purchased by the Kellogg Company for $600 million.

Class of 2008: Mark Campbell

Mark was an ensemble member of The Second City etc. 43rd revue and of The Second City National Touring Company. He also performed with The Improvised Shakespeare Company at iO Chicago

Photo by Ian McLaren

Class of 2008: John Shurna

The all-time leading scorer at Northwestern University in men's basketball.

Pictured, left, John playing in Spain

Class of 2009: Chris Watt

Chris was drafted in 2014 and was an NFL Offensive lineman for the San Diego Chargers until 2016. He then signed with the New Orleans Saints. He retired from the NFL in 2017.

Did we miss someone? Please contact us: steve_wiersum@glenbard.org

The Glenbard West High School Historic Society: Allie Dahlgren and Grace Davidson

There needs to be a special mention of Allie and Grace in this book. In the beginning of the book, I mentioned how the GWHS Historic Society sprang into existence. A chance meeting and conversation became a full-blown club with meetings and everything. Our motto: "Pizza. Pop. Preservation." Allie started things and jump started the group. Grace is the one who insisted it keeping going. Whenever we would run into each other in the hall, Grace would ask, "When is the next Historic Society meeting?" I would feel embarrassed if I didn't have a reply other than, "Um, let me check my calendar." Eventually, we would just meet the first Friday of every month. It was just easier that way.

So, thank you to Allie for getting things going. Thank you to Grace for being so persistent in keeping things going. I owe both of you so much. Most of all, I am grateful that you both cared so much about this wonderful school to invest so much time and energy to make sure the story didn't remain buried.

At left, Joe Carlton, Glenbard High School graduate and author of the book, *As the Backs go Tearing By*, a detailed history of Glenbard's football story. Grace Davidson, the second GWHS Historic Society club president, presents him with and official Glenbard West Historical Society t-shirt—a must wear on all Fridays.

The Very First GWHS Historic Society: 2013-2014

The First GWHS Historic Society Club Members: 2013-2014
Taylor Moen, Allie Dahlgren, Bridgid Nannenhorn, Kelsey Newman

A Growing GWHS Historic Society Meets in May 2014

Meg Malone

Allie Dahlgren

Lizzy Flemming

Rachel Warren

Brigid Nannenhorn

Natalie Kutcher

Elise Olson

Gabriella Bower

The 2014 GWHS Historic Society

Left, a photo from the 1940 Pinnacle yearbook. Below, a photo of the 2017 GWHS Historic Society taken in the exact same spot, 77 years later. We're not up in the tower, but we're close. And the view is amazing!

Narratives from Alumni

We are hoping to gather multiple narratives from our alumni of their time on the Hilltop. Notice how fast time flies! We do not have any narratives from the early years—and I fear we never will.

For the 3rd edition of this book, we would welcome more stories to fill out our 100 years. Please feel free to submit your Glenbard Memory to steve_wiersum@glenbard.org. 300-500 words is a great length.

No submissions from the Class of 1916-1919, 1920-1929, or 1930-39

Harold "Snub" Pritchard, Class of 1946

My memories of having attended Glenbard High School are nothing but great. I must admit my true interest while attending GHS were Sports and Girls. I am afraid academics came in 3rd. I can honestly say those four years were some the best four years of my life.

To this day when I go to a GWHS football game with my fellow "Old Codgers," we spend the majority of our time there talking about our days at GHS. At the time, boys' sports had a lightweight and a heavyweight division in football and basketball. How lucky for boys like me. As a lightweight, I got to play four years of both football and basketball.

Because of these sports I developed friendships that are still true to this day. I couldn't wait to get to school each day during the two seasons. My fondest memory is our basketball team (which was made up of guys who had been playing together both on and off the gym since 7th grade) won the championship as seniors losing only one game.

Being in school during WWII was a unique experience. Concerns and worries about the war made it very difficult on teachers, students and Mr. Biester as we had to see the seniors going through their senior year knowing they were destined to have to enter the war. As a result, it was very hard for my fellow students to really care about studies, etc. Our teachers were so attached to their graduating seniors and we under-classmates could feel the grief of our teachers.

As to the girls, if we weren't thinking about sports, it was about the girls. It was amazing how getting to school early, so you could spend time with your true love in front of her locker was misinterpreted to mean you just couldn't wait to get to class. Heart Hop was a dance where girls asked the boys to the dance and of course we all pretended like we didn't care if we didn't get selected.

As I look back, I have to give a tremendous amount of credit to the teachers and Principal Biester for their handling those very difficult years during the war.

In summary, attending Glenbard, for me, was such a wonderful experience and because it was, I and a few others who still live in Glen Ellyn never cease to somehow bring up our years at GHS whenever we meet.

Lester Munson, Class of 1958

In the second session of a course entitled English Composition in the fall of 1957, a tall and imposing Glenbard teacher stood before her class, ordered her students to take out pen and paper, and told them she would "dictate" three paragraphs to them. Their job for the next few minutes, she said, was to write down her dictation, word for word. The students, all seniors including me, were puzzled. A dictation? None of them had ever before experienced anything like it.

The smooth and highly descriptive sentences that the teacher, Gladys Kronsagen dictated to us seemed to be taken from the National Geographic. At age 17, I was an A student and was beginning to think that I wanted to be a writer. I hoped to do well in the course, and I knew it was known as the most challenging in the school. I was listening closely when she ended a sentence with the phrase, "the vast steppes of Russia." I wrote on my paper, "the vast steps of Russia." When Mrs. Kronsagen handed my paper back to me marked with a "B," I was shocked. When she pointed out my mistake to the entire class, I was mortified.

It was the last mistake I made in the class. I worked diligently on each assignment thereafter and proofread every submission again and again. I wrote a research paper with dozens of footnotes on investment clubs that were then becoming popular. It earned an A and prompted Mrs. Kronsagen and her husband, a chemistry teacher at Glenbard, to start their own club to study the stock market.

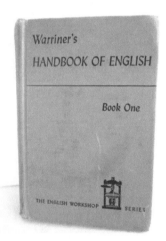

(Pictured, right, the book that Lester Munson used in his English class. He saved it and still has it to this day. It has stayed with him for 60 years.)

At my request, Mrs. Kronsagen wrote a recommendation in support of my college applications. I've lost the letter, but it was a basis for my admission to Princeton University. In orientation week at Princeton, I was informed that because I came from an unfamiliar and doubtful public high school, I must take an examination in composition and grammar. Approximately 150 of 750 freshmen sat for the test. I did well on the exam, so well that my advisor informed me that my grade was the best of the year. I wrote to my parents about it, and they passed the test result on to Fred Biester who read portions of my letter about the test to the school on the public address system during the morning announcements. In the next year, Princeton admitted three young men from Glenbard.

Gladys Kronsagen (pictured, right) was the best teacher I had at Glenbard. She was stern, demanding, and fair. She was so accomplished in her scholarly specialty that she was named as an editor of the English language handbook that we used on class. I have kept the book with me for 60 years. I have consulted it from time to time during my 30 years as a paid, professional sportswriter at *The National Sports Daily*, *Sports Illustrated*, and ESPN.

Edward Sanderson, Class of 1966

My first year there was Mr. Biester's last. A sad day for GWHS. There is an important person left out of this history. Mr. Richard Whitecotton. (Pictured, right. Later he became Dr. Whitecotton. He became the Choir Director I believe around 1960 and shortly after taking that position became the head of the music department which flourished under his leadership. While I was a student there in those early 60s one fourth of the student population was part of the Choir and Chorus'. The Christmas and Spring Concerts were fantastic and every year an album was made of the Spring Concert. You might want to think of adding this to the history. "Mr. W" had a huge influence on so many students at GWHS! Including me!

Marcy Nichols, Class of 1976

It was fall of 1973, my freshman year. I remember sitting in the cafeteria with all the freshman girls one night in the beginning of the year. I was at a table with a friend talking and not really paying attention. We were there to vote for 2 freshman girls to be on Pep Club Council.

My friend said to me; "Marcy they just called your name!" I wasn't sure, but they had and I was shocked by this. I had no idea what it meant to be on in pep club. I couldn't believe my peers had voted me in! We immediately had to do a skit with the other council members for a total of eight. Two members from each class. I was still shy.

Pep Club was, what I call, the "silent cheerleaders." I learned that first year we were the ones who made the posters for all of the Hilltopper team games and hung them everywhere in the school we could! We sold hotdogs, popcorn and food at all the games, including the away games. We traveled with the teams. We were the ones who toilet papered the team player's homes late at night on Thursday's for pep rally Friday's.

We also had our own uniforms we would wear every Friday just like the cheerleaders and the Topperettes did. Every year we would go shopping as a council and get what we liked, in mandatory green and white.

Thursday night, homecoming week of 1974, we had a busy night ahead of us and knew it would be well after midnight before we were done with our silent cheerleading chores. We were allowed into the boys locker-room every year to decorate it for them. This particular year while we were putting up the banners, posters, and crepe paper, we heard the door to the outside open. Now, no one knew we were there that night, so we all looked to see what it was. It was dark and as we looked, we saw a male, probably a fellow classmate, dressed in a pink two-piece negligee with a nylon over his face and head!
We were so scared we all screamed and crawled up the sides of the lockers to get up top! As high and as far as we could get from this frightening person! This was our natural reaction and then he was gone. It took us a minute to get the courage to get down and open the door to see if he was really gone or not. What a relief he was nowhere in sight!

After we got over our nervousness, we finished what we were doing in the locker room. We knew we had much more to do that night. We finished the night about 4am by toilet papering the outside of the school that night. So, if you ever wondered who it was that took care of all the posters and toilet papering of the houses and school it was us: Pep Club Council.

Amy Weliver Bendigkeit, Class of 1979

Photos by James Derk

Slowly, unrolling the shiny aluminum foil, I stretch it over 6-plus-feet to wrap around the huge hoop that the football team will charge through as they bound on to the field.

"You think we have enough foil, or do we need to go back to Cee Bees for more?" Janine wonders aloud.

I'm sure it's enough. We laugh as we work. Of all the hoops we created, I love this one best. It's shiny and bright. (Just like us!) It's homecoming. GLENBARD WEST HOMECOMING.

"We have spirit...YES WE DO!"

And how could we not? This place is steeped in tradition. And those of us that were in a place of knowing—played in it. Lapped it up. Yes, REVELED in the forest green and white.

When you have a high school that resembles a stoic castle on top of a hill...complete with ivy covered walls. You know it's going to be good!

HILLTOPPERS . . . HITTERS. When asked to write A MEMORY about GBW, I cannot come back to any particular story but only to the incredible FEELING of synergy I/we experienced through my high school years. A KNOWING that this place was special.

A belonging.

"We got pride on our side..."

Homecoming itself captures it best: weeks of building floats for the parade in damp garages, making ghosties to stuff between the chicken wire while we laughed and sang along to tunes on the '70's radio. (There could have been beer involved- wink)

Playing pranks on each other. Learning "the hustle "in honors gym class. Decorating lockers. The funny skits during the pep rally with the team and teachers fair game targets. T.P.-ing houses. (learned later the guys really resented having to do the clean up!)

(My mom- seriously - you have to work to pay off buying toilet paper!)

The parade. (Choir float RULES! And hey! GAA, we know how much your Dads designed and built your float!) quite the rivalry.

The football game starts in this magical setting with Lake Ellyn as a backdrop. Gold helmets recently introduced. Pre-Duchon field days.

The sharp synchronization of our arms doing cheers while watching my huge yellow mum (surely from the green sale) lose all its petals and falls on the track.

Watching an admired friend crowned homecoming queen standing with her proud Papa. The victory bell ringing.

Then it's on to the homecoming dance. Dresses purchased at Flemings or Lord and Taylor. (Yes, I passed your date a note in science class to be sure to order a nosegay NOT the wristlet corsage.) The getting ready. Picture parties and realizing how far we've come in being more comfortable with ourselves at this time by senior year. (Come on! A powder blue leisure suit gives every guy a reason to stand tall!)

Tons of balloons for the homecoming dance. (Too much glitter on the steps leading down to the cloak room. Slid down the steps, making a mortified girl with me! I bounce pretty good!) Dancing. . . after all we ARE staying alive! "picking stars!

The after party. Hey . . . the basements were dark. You know who you are . . . you know what you did!

Wink.

Lori Scott Pikkaart, Class of 1989

Somehow over the passage of time, those four, formative high school years become enlarged in the memory. Our teenage selves were emerging from childhood, forging a new consciousness about the world around us, advancing in social skills, adjusting to a maturing physique, encountering new emotions, and just trying to find footing in an adult world.

My grandmother, the daughter of Polish immigrants, always told me that I lived a charmed life. She was right. Glen Ellyn and Glenbard West are like no other places in the world; there's something special about those coordinates on planet earth. Even Hollywood's location scouts agreed. If I want to go back in time to the affluent Chicago suburbs in the '80s, I can just tune in to any John Hughes movie. Or watch "Lucas."

For those who desired to grasp it, we truly received a quality education in that stately old castle, the "dump on the hump." Of course, we learned a lot of academic facts, but I managed to glean extra wisdom. There was Mrs. Carrel the Algebra teacher telling us that "Math is a pattern." Mr. Holmes the Trigonometry expert was always encouraging us with, "It's a great day to be alive!" My sweet Spanish teacher, Mrs. Jurgens warned new drivers, telling us what she told her own children, that "a car is a weapon."

Lessons from two teachers still resonate. I used to write John London-esque fiction. Mrs. Weinstock in the English department was kind enough to look over my writings on her own time, gently sharing her suggested edits with me. It's humbling to have someone point out areas where you can improve on something you've already poured your heart into—that feeling of being edited for the first time. As a magazine editor today, I take those feelings into account when I edit laypersons for what is probably their first time.

In art class, Mr. Schwartz noticed my talents, encouraging me to pursue it as a career. Referring to more academic pursuits, I replied, "No, I want to do something that uses my brain." He laughed! I did end up circling back to art, my happy place, first as a graphic designer and these days as a fine artist doing commissioned works. I reached out to thank him several years ago, and he still fondly remembered our conversation. My mom thought I needed to round out my college

resume by joining the yearbook staff. Under the leadership of Mr. CopperSmith (shown left), I learned the basics of good layout and design, typography and photography. It was there that I met one of my closest friends, photographer Brian Fugiel, who ended up taking me to the senior prom (Sadly, he passed away suddenly in 2006.). My reluctant acceptance of my mom's advice ended up blessing me even to this day.

Glenbard West is a place full of traditions. Every year the beautiful campus is pranked with For Sale signs, but I don't think there is anyone who would buy it—too priceless.

Richard Slisz, Class of 1992 and Lori Heidorn Slisz, Class of 1993.

The picture, right, was taken for prom. The bottom picture is from their wedding. Richard and Lori met at GWHS.

Text by Lori

My life at Glenbard West High school started in 1990, I was a freshman and my first day of school I walked up to Richard (who is my husband now) and said that I would never date someone as scary looking as him. He was wearing a three-piece suit, trench coat, carrying a briefcase, and his hair was pulled back in a ponytail down to his butt. I don't remember him again until my senior year.

I was quite all during high school--which was quite funny because I am a loud Italian that you could never shut up. My best friend at the time was dating Richards best friend and they all told me that I knew him, but I had no idea who he was until I saw him, and freshman year went flashing through my head.

We started dating November 20, 1992, and that is when I finally become known at Glenbard West. I made the mistake of telling one of the deans who I was dating. Now, when Richard was at school, he was well... how do say… well known by the deans. Now almost once a week I was called over the PA system to report to the dean's office. The dean would talk to me about my grades and/or why I keep ditching classes. I would not change a thing except I would have liked to have been more involved with school activities and not be so shy.

Richard and I have been together for 27 years and will have been married for 20 years in 2019. You never know who you will fall in love with. You can say that I met my husband when I was just a little girl. My mom and Richard's mom both bowled on the same day, Tuesday mornings, at Brunswick bowling alley.

Our moms would put us in the day care there. My mom would get me all kinds of snacks. This little boy would not leave me alone, so I told my mom, and my mom told me that I should share my snacks. That little boy would drive me crazy he would follow me everywhere and he would through his toys at me.

Many years later, that same little boy and I became high school sweethearts. I am proud to say, that little boy is now my husband! The crazy part is that we were married about 11 years before we figured it out. Life is short. Live it to the fullest!

Molly Hernandez, Class of 2015

Pride. Tradition. Excellence. This has been the slogan for Glenbard West since before my time. As a member of the 2015 graduating class, I believe that the community was undeniably committed to inspiring all learners.

Every spring, hundreds of students are recognized at award ceremonies for their achievements in the department, school, state, and nation for their incredible achievements. These ceremonies showed me how important it is to recognize all forms of achievement. While getting an 'A'' in AP European History is certainly quite a feat, we must also celebrate the aspiring chef who won a national cooking competition, the most improved driver's education student, the first-generation high school student who passed a Technology Center of DuPage class, and the color guard team who went to state.

Because the pride is evident in students, staff, alumni, and the community, West is flooded with traditions that demonstrate this. The homecoming bonfire and parade with a winning Glenbard Latino Association float anchored my HS experience. Watching the band march down the hill pre-game, the football team sounding the bell after each win, or the student council president in a turkey suit were close behind.

The culminating senior activities including the pre-first day senior walk, tour-de-West, and the final picnic have been passed down from generation to generation. None of these could happen without West's commitment to excellence.

It may be the excellent way they mainstream special needs students into the countless student organizations. Or it may be West's academic rigor as I was shocked at my college preparation and attribute much of this to the phenomenal staff.

I was consistently challenged and pushed by teachers and other students alike. West embodies the true essence of pride, tradition, and excellence and inspires me to live with those qualities.

From Grace Bouton, Class of 2018

I remember walking through the fluorescent-lit halls my freshman year in awe of the layers of history embedded in the school's walls. I would often daydream in class, imagining everything from the poodle skirts that once graced the tile floor to fresh-perms teased to the heavens. I knew I was a part of something special, but I could never fathom just how much the next four years would mean to me.

My time at West was full of ups and downs — and I'm not talking about the millions of stairs I trekked over four years. Had you asked me about West while I was in high school, I most likely would've given you an answer about AP tests and an upcoming assignment I was scrambling to finish. But looking at it now, it was so much more than that. It was in those halls where I experienced my first love, my first heartbreak. I aced tests, I failed some too. I made lifelong friends, I lost some along the way.

Call it cliché, but without West, I wouldn't have some of the memories I hold most dear to my heart. I wouldn't know what it meant to stop by the auditorium on a Friday night and re-enacting songs from *Hamilton* with Molly and Davidson. I wouldn't understand the adrenaline of sneaking into the crawl-space above the cafeteria with GT (if anyone of authority is reading this, you should really lock that.) I wouldn't have written a musical with my best friend G-Cent — and even have it produced in the Black Box theatre. But most importantly, I would have no inkling of how precious a glimpse of four years can be.

I know my ring of the Victory Bell is one of thousands, and my spot on the bleachers for Saturday game-days will be filled for years to come, but my time at West engraved memories that will remain. I can only hope that someday, in some classroom, a girl will daydream of our ripped skinny jeans running to class and our lip-gloss stained smiles laughing about the latest Tweet. If only walls could talk; I wish they could share just all the fun we had.

Topics we are still researching

If you have any information or corrections about the following topics, please contact us.

First, as we celebrated Black History month in February 2018, we wondered about the first African-American students to be named as King and Queen for Homecoming, Heart Hop, or Prom. Here is what our research has shown so far. Is this correct?

The First Black Heart Hop King was Antoine Watkins in1993. He is show here with his date, Kathy Pollard.

The First Black Prom Queen was Helen Steele in 1991. She is shown here with her date, Prom King Paul Taylor.

We are also looking for a picture of school board president Louis J. Thiele. He served in Glenbard's earliest history.

Contact us

If you have a story or a thought or a suggestion or correction or memorabilia, please reach out and contact us. Steve Wiersum can be emailed at steve_wiersum@glenbard.org
GWHS Main Switchboard: 630-469-8600.

Facebook pages:
- Glenbard West High School Friends
- Glenbard West Historic Society

YouTube Channel
- Glenbard West Historical Society Playlist

Pictured, the 2017-2018 GWHS Historic Society. The group's mission that year: to try and bring back the varsity cardigan sweater.

Do you have any Glenbard West memorabilia that you would like to donate to our GWHS Museum? If so, reach out to us and we can make plans to have it framed, mounted, and preserved.

Printed in the United States
By Bookmasters